MOMENTUM

To Lori,

Dream Big ♡

Seth Lenny

Dec 2020

MOMENTUM

WHERE MINDSET MEETS STRATEGY:
SEVEN STEPS TO START AND KEEP
MOMENTUM IN BUSINESS FOREVER

SETH LEWIS

NEW DEGREE PRESS

MOMENTUM
*Where mindset meets strategy: seven steps to start
and keep momentum in business forever*

ISBN
978-1-63676-629-4   *Paperback*
978-1-63676-253-1   *Kindle Ebook*
978-1-63676-246-3   *Digital Ebook*

I'm the luckiest guy in the world. To my beautiful wife Janelle and daughter Brooke, I never knew life could be this sweet. To my mom, thank you for always supporting me. To my brothers, you have turned into amazing men. I'm proud of you. I love you all. To my mentors—I am forever grateful to you for making an impact in my life. I am indebted to you and know that I will pass it on just like you did to me.

CONTENTS

Mindset will change your momentum forever.

—SETH LEWIS

INTRODUCTION

I was about to go into a meeting when the President of the United States called...

I grew up in Grantville, a small town in Pennsylvania famous among the locals for the annual fireman's carnival.

As a kid, I always wanted to play football. I would watch NFL football games on TV on Sunday afternoons and then go outside and replicate the plays. I would throw the ball up in the air as high as I possibly could and fight to see it as it came down with the shining sun. When I would catch it, the "play" would be live. I would run, dodge, and juke all the imaginary players coming to tackle me. As I had a few final steps left to reach the end zone, I had one player who always seemed to get me. As I was falling to the hard ground, I would stretch out the ball to cross the goal line, making a touchdown. Not only was this a touchdown, but it was also the score that my team needed to win the game! I replicated plays like these hundreds of times.

After watching and replicating the professional players, I asked my mom if there was a team I could play on. She wasn't so sure about that, asking, "Are you sure you want to play on a team? Football is rough, and you may get hurt."

Tryouts were coming up at the local park. As a kid, "tryouts" usually mean you show up and you get to play. We took the short drive to the park down the street only for the coach to tell me I was too big. I grew to about six feet tall by sixth grade and was always the tallest in my class throughout grade school. I thought I was destined for the NFL or NBA with my size. I would not be able to play football all of my youth years because I was a giant kid. In life, we consistently run into challenges or blocks, but how we handle them either leads to our success, which I call momentum, or failure, which I call negative momentum.

Fast forward a few years. I was finally able to play football in high school after some strong convincing from my friend Josh Gregor. The block that happened turned into an opportunity as I was well-rested and ready to make an impact. It went really well—so well that I was recruited by Penn State Football my senior year.

Coach Larry Johnson was the coach who brought my family and me to visit. Parents have a way of embarrassing their kids. I remember my mom asking about Coach Johnson's family and what his kids did. I was so embarrassed. Did my mom not know that Coach Johnson's son was Larry Johnson Jr.—the NFL's leading rusher that year?

What was I most excited about on my visit was my meeting with Coach Joe Paterno. Joe Paterno was a head coach of the Penn State Football team. He was one of the all-time winningest coaches in college football history, with 409 wins. As this meeting got closer, my excitement was building. Then I got a call from Coach Johnson. He told me that my meeting with Coach Paterno had to be canceled. President George W. Bush called Coach Paterno and asked him to ride with him in his motorcade. There was an event in State College, Pennsylvania, and the president requested that he ride along.

There went my meeting. I didn't realize how much I wanted that meeting until it wasn't there anymore. What impressed me most? As I sat in Coach Paterno's office feeling completely dejected, I received a call from him. He was with the President of the United States, but he still took time out of their visit to call me—on the president's phone!

This moment changed my momentum forever. Initially, it was what I call a block. At the time, I didn't understand it, but it actually accelerated my momentum. During life, we all have moments like this where what we want most is derailed by some unexpected event. How we handle these events is how we drive toward true momentum.

Some of us may have been taught that momentum is driven by luck, and we have never questioned or examined that more deeply until now. The good news is you can strategically build momentum for yourself or your organization.

Southwest Airlines is a perfect example of how an organization chose to strategically build momentum through a simple approach.

In 1981, Herb Kelleher became the CEO of Southwest airlines after being its attorney for years. Herb knew that airlines overall were losing money, and he intended to change that with Southwest. Herb kept Southwest's offering very simple.[1] Initially, Southwest airlines only set up flights between Dallas, San Antonio, and Houston, before expanding to other cities.

Herb's other main focus was the people of Southwest Airlines. He is famous for saying, "Take care of your employees first, and your customers second." He believed that the power in Southwest's financial success was held in its people. As of 2020, Southwest Airlines has reported forty-seven consecutive years of profitability. Herb stated in an interview with *60 Minutes*, "We have the most productive people in the industry and they are proud of what they do."[2] He challenged what everyone believed to be true about the airline industry and how it had to be done. Herb Kelleher proved an airline could have low cost and great customer service while still making a profit![3]

Just like Southwest, this book is going to challenge what you believe around gaining and keeping traction in business. I ask that you keep an open mind and question what limiting beliefs you may have. We all have them, and I guarantee they are holding you back, just like the limiting beliefs from Southwest's competing airlines. I want this book to challenge you to take action and be profitable for the next forty-seven years. To never be stuck again. To have the wild success that you deserve.

---

1   "The 60 Minutes interview: Southwest's Herb Kelleher," *60 Minutes Rewind*, January 4, 2019, video, 11:01.

2   "Southwest Airlines Reports 47th Consecutive Year of Profitability," *Investor Relations*, Southwest Airlines Co., January 23, 2020.

3   "Southwest's Herb Kelleher," *60 Minutes Rewind*.

And who am I to help you do that?

I have spent the last seventeen years as an entrepreneur learning business through the University of Hard Knocks. I also have an Executive MBA from Villanova University. I have owned eight companies, developed an app, wrote a book; I own real estate and, at the end of the day, have a passion for helping people in business win. I have experienced momentum by challenging the concept that momentum happens by chance. I set out on a journey in 2019 to own the topic of momentum. As I researched the topic, I realized that no one owned the space. I want to be the guy synonymous with momentum. I want to own the topic of momentum just like John Maxwell owns leadership.

My most rewarding experience has been motivating teams and leaders to be the best versions of themselves. In turn, helping others has led to personal satisfaction as well as financial gains not only for me but for those whom I have been able to work with. As a leader, reading this book will not only change your life but impact those whom you interact with daily. Momentum is an investment you probably have been missing as a CEO, leader, or business owner.

Momentum is a force that builds quickly when you get the correct pieces aligned, and it compounds quickly. If you want your business or organization to pick up speed, build a culture that drives engagement as well as long term customer satisfaction and profitability. Momentum is the vehicle that ties all of this together! True momentum occurs when you begin with a holistic point of view of your inner self and how you lead and make decisions. Momentum builds as you understand your way of thinking and create a new data set through which to evaluate decisions while incorporating your team to outline your newfound strategy. As a leader, once you adopt this holistic approach to momentum, the impact will change how you show up mentally to work. It will change how you show up for your customers and, most importantly, it will change how you show up for your family.

I believe there are seven steps to starting and sustaining momentum, and I will highlight specific examples in each step in the book from leaders around the globe. I want everyone to know any company can implement them as long as they are committed to their success and follow each step.

The seven steps are the following:

- Awareness/Mindset
- ROI/Value
- Culture
- Strategy
- Leadership
- Energy
- Measure and Adjust

I will cover these in more detail in the book. As we go through the seven steps, pay attention to the order. Just like the order of operations in a math problem, when completed in this order, the force of momentum compounds. I will share numerous examples from my experience and those of not only small businesses but also global brands that embraced these elements to drive explosive momentum. This book is through the lens of business; however, if you are not a business owner or leader, my seven steps can also be applied to your life personally. Please follow me on this journey and be a part of it. Share it. Like it. Until now, no one else has accepted this challenge. I have, and I'm excited to share it with you. You have the keys to it. You simply have to unlock it.

In a very short time, my Start the Mo (Momentum) has become explosive, and my process has unlocked what has always been there! The impact has been in all of my organizations. As you follow me, I want you to experience explosive momentum in your life wherever you are. Thanks for coming along.

It's time... Let's Get it!

CHAPTER 1

AWARENESS AND MINDSET

——

We all have a blind spot, and it's shaped exactly like us.

—JUNOT DIAZ

My wife said, "Your breath stinks."

After being blindsided by her comment, I asked, "Are you serious?" I could tell from her look when I opened up to respond she was serious.

She said, "Yes."

Wait a minute. Had I been living my whole life with stinky breath? This was immediately my biggest problem to solve. Why didn't anyone tell me this? I pictured all the customers I met with, all the presentations I gave. I thought about my staff and the reputation I must have. Then my mind turned to health. I asked myself, "Did something change with my health? Maybe I should go to the doctor and get checked." Throughout my life, personal hygiene has always been super important to me. I'm the guy who takes eight pairs of underwear for a two-night trip. I just view it as unacceptable to, for lack of a better term, stink.

As I continued to look into what changed. I realized that a few weeks ago, I started the keto diet. As I researched, I came across this from *Healthline*. "Many people on ketogenic diets and similar diets, such as the Atkins diet, report that their breath takes on a fruity smell. This is caused by elevated ketone levels. The specific culprit is acetone, a ketone that exits the body in your urine and breath."[4]

This explained it! Whew! I could accept this because I was able to then do something about it. First, I was made aware by my wife. Now that I was aware that my breath was funky, I could do something about it.

As I continued to think about how this situation connected to momentum, I realized this was the perfect example of the foundation of momentum. Without awareness of the problem, you cannot work on a solution. The greatest organizations, leaders, and business owners have terrific awareness and act before problems arise. They also recognize the importance of having outside feedback through mentors, coaches, boards, or any other perspectives that can help identify blind spots. Without awareness, momentum is stalled.

---

4   Rudy Mawer, "10 Signs and Symptoms That You're in Ketosis," *Healthline*, August 2, 2018.

Like the example above, the problem most businesses have is they do not know their "breath stinks." Many do not have someone to tell them their breath stinks. They operate with this "stinky" breath, and it is killing their business. Once they can see the problem, they can begin to work on it. They can start the journey to find the solution. In this chapter, we look at both awareness and mindset as they combine to make a strong foundation to gain explosive momentum.

In my story, once I was aware, I had a choice. My first choice would have been to deny there was a problem. Many businesses do this, and they will never experience sustainable momentum. The second choice I had was to accept that I had something going on that needed attention. I was uncomfortable and did not like the thought, but it was true. This is where mindset comes into play. How I determine to handle the information that is presented will be directly correlated to the amount of momentum I have and gain as my journey continues. I chose to accept the feedback, and my mindset was 100 percent committed to finding a solution at all costs. Businesses that do this begin the journey to a life of abundance and unlock the doors to success that they have not experienced before.

BECOMING AWARE OF WHAT'S STOPPING YOU

At the time, I was like many other business owners. I never connected mindset and strategy. I had worked with many consultants and tried to combine what I learned from one book with the next one. I would try to talk to people and blend some magical solution that never happened.

Then I spoke with Geeta Nadkarni and she helped me connect all the information that I had learned over the years. First, I must say I have had so many people help me along my journey, and this doesn't take away from any of that. She simply helped me tie all of it together through the power of mindset. It became the foundation of my program and inspired me to help others in a similar way. She and her team were able to help me see where I kept fumbling.

Imagine running a marathon and always having your body cramp around mile eighteen and not being able to finish. When you don't make it to the finish, you have two options. The first is to never try to run a marathon again because of fear that your body will do it again. The second is to train smarter and harder and improve your nutrition to try to overcome the challenge. Option two was for me. Try to continually improve. The problem was I kept trying new "stuff." Part of this was my nature or mindset, and it caused me to continue to cramp at my mile eighteen. Up until this point in time, I had success, but I had just as many challenges.

I couldn't figure out why I couldn't get the brakes fully off. Sometimes it felt like I was driving down the highway with the emergency brake on. My car wanted to go but something continued to hold it back. My brake in my career up until this point was my mindset. You will see as you read through the seven steps to start and sustain momentum how we build off the foundation of awareness. You will also see when you get to the end how it connects back to help you keep momentum forever. This chapter is important as it will be the foundation of how we build.

THE POWER OF AWARENESS... AND THE MIND

"I remember being in labor, in the worst pain I've ever been in my life, and remember thinking, 'How is my body doing this?' I remember this feeling of just moving out of my own way. How did I have so much power in this body and have not known it my whole life?" That is the moment Geeta Nadkarni changed forever.

She said this when I asked her how she came to connect the power of mindset with her work. Her career started at twelve with her first paid writing gig, and her career followed into writing and television. Her work has been featured all over the media, in multiple countries including *Forbes*, *The New York Times*, *Entrepreneur*, *Huffington Post*, ABC, CBC, CTV, and many more. Today, she helps coaches and consultants take their expertise online and create a highly supportive, profitable, scalable, and fulfilling program.

It wasn't always easy. In those painful moments of childbirth with her son, she realized that she needed to be home with him. She had a conflict: "At the time, my income was important for our family, so I couldn't just take off... but I did. I woke up after having my son and said, 'I'm not going back to the 9-5.' Then for me, full-blown panic hit! Most people run back to what they've known but for me, I'm stubborn so I was just like, I'm going to figure this out. No one understood what I was doing and never did at the moment. It got so bad I had to turn my phone on airplane mode because my family was blowing me up asking when I was going to get a 'job.' This went on for months while people were telling me I was irresponsible. 'You have a mortgage, a baby and you want to make money online?!' When I would take my son for walks and with my eyes open, I would just pray and talk to the universe to help show me the way. 'I'm not giving up.' For me, I joke that the universe talks to me through Facebook."

She continued, "I haven't gained from every investment, but they were all pieces of my journey. I learned in my journey how to win. Winning is not the hustle energy that I used to think it was. Now I connect to how I want to feel. Any outcome that you want is ultimately going to lead to a feeling, and I focus on the feeling I want."

"Once your mindset changes, everything on the outside will change along with it."

—STEVE MARABOLI

IS MINDSET JUST A BUZZWORD?

Everything starts with mindset, but it's become one of those words that has lost its magic because of the number of people who use it. It can also mean different things to different people. Geeta said, "One of my clients, at the core, did not know what she wanted. She kept taking courses and certifications, which she passed with no problem, but she still felt stuck and was not satisfied. When she joined my program, she realized she was confused. We uncovered that in her childhood she was not allowed to do what she wanted. This came from her caregivers. She had no idea that it was her programming or mindset from her childhood that was allowing her to always do the tactical parts but never permitting herself to put the pieces together to gain her true desire. Specifically, what was holding her back was fear of getting what she really wanted. We went deep into this and helped her release those limiting stories. Once we did that, honestly everything that she had collected along her journey suddenly became useful in a way that it hadn't been before."

As I listened to Geeta's example, I realized this is so true. Many of us struggle but do not know why we are struggling. Holding us back is usually not the program or course, but something within us—not our mentors. If you read that above example and said, "How could she not know? Why would she do that?" you may be a perfect example of someone who may be missing the deeper level behind why you are making the decisions you are making. We know that the way we process information, the way we view the world, is all created throughout our life. We have a lens that we not only view life through but make our business decisions through too. The problem is we never do the work to go back and reevaluate our lens. If it's working, we don't look any further. If it's not working, we blame it on something else.

I can relate to Geeta's example because that was me. I dove deep into my own narrative to help me understand why my momentum would always eventually fall apart. Once I understood my own limiting beliefs and worked to evaluate my lens, I changed that "prescription" and could see twenty-twenty. It was like a business revival! I truly believe without doing a deep dive to understand my mindset, I would have been on the up and down cycle for the rest of my life. Instead, everything that I learned throughout my life has come back in a powerful way, leading to explosive momentum in a very short time.

THE MIND AND THE PERFECT EXCUSE

Mindset is what controls and leads to limiting beliefs like imposter syndrome, why you can or can't charge premium rates, and why you may not believe you can get staff, sales, or even retain customers. I remember my initial coaching call with Geeta. If I made a decision on the spot to hire her as a coach, it would save me $5,000. I had all the information and knew it was the solution that I needed, but I hesitated because we are conditioned to wait.

From day one, my indecision cost me money. It was the first time it was laid out plain as day. Our minds give us every reason why we should not take action. The excuses against speak up louder than those that are for the solution. *What if it doesn't work? I have to check with my wife or husband. I'll wait until I take care of...* The excuses go on. If this solution is going to help bring clarity to your life, what spouse wouldn't support that? If this solution will help you achieve your goal faster, why are you delaying it?

The cost of a program that works is nothing compared to the impact of bringing all your knowledge to life again. I learned one of my most valuable lessons when I declined to commit that day on the phone. Geeta and her team called out every one of my objections until I had nothing to say. "I need to think about it."

They responded, "What do you need to think about?"

I was caught. I ended up saying, "I just don't want to commit to spending that amount of money on the spot."

I agreed it was the solution for me, and I knew it would work, but I was still stuck. This resembled areas of my business that I didn't make swift strong confident decisions, and it became more obvious that I was struggling with mindset. I had no clue. It was a Friday when I asked to think about it over the weekend. They told me confidently that waiting would cost me an additional $5,000 and asked me if it was worth it. I said yes.

That conversation exposed some of my weaknesses, and I realized that I had a lot to work on. I had a follow-up call the next Tuesday. I knew I was going to pay the extra $5,000, and I was ready to do it. I didn't want a discount, and I knew they weren't going to give me one. They were confident in their solution and understood their value. I also made a commitment that that was going to be me in the future. Geeta and her team were firm, fair, and clear. I decided that I was going to commit to that journey. One of my mentors, Dan Eichenlaub, who has been one of my biggest fans and supporters, had been in my ear to adopt premium pricing for years. With all my heart I tried, but I never realized it was my own mindset that was holding me back.

HAVING BLIND SPOTS MAKES YOU NORMAL

What happens when the best heart surgeon in the world needs heart surgery? They have to find a heart surgeon. You could be the smartest person and best surgeon, but you can't operate on yourself. This leads to imposter syndrome in many business owners.

You can't do for yourself what you may be able to do very well for others. This leads to thoughts of not wanting to promote yourself because you have or had the same problem as your client.

Some of these statements you may have to reread because they do make you think. If you were to try to perform surgery on yourself, you don't have the normal perspective that you would if you were working on someone else. You are not able to see things the same way you are used to. As a surgeon, you still have to be fully embodied in what you teach, and you can help people through the process if you had to because you know it so well, but you still can't help yourself. This same principle is why my Momentum U program has grown so rapidly. I've been on this journey and have experienced the pain. I know what it feels like, and that is why I have been able to help create change in people's lives through their business. That is why I still have my own coaches, because I need their help when I "need surgery."

THE GLITCH IN HUMAN CONSCIOUSNESS

I was asking a prospective client about their target customer, and they said everyone who has money. I knew there was a lot of work to do. This is normal for most business people and leaders to say. We are all on 80 percent autopilot. We do relatively the same thing every day. We drive the same roads, use the same coffee mug, put our keys in the same spot. This happens until something shakes it up or disrupts our normal flow. We ask the same questions when we meet someone and generally have the same responses.

This becomes a huge problem in business because we never take the time to dive deep and ask the next-level question to get to the root. Many leaders keep looking for a new solution instead of mastering the basics, diving deep into the root cause or simple solution. As humans, many of us are not good at repetition. If you are a high achiever, this is probably you. You are ready for the next book, next course, next coach, etc. The problem with how many of us think is once we hear the solution, we think the problem is fixed, and we never fully implement it until we see the next solution and then we jump there.

Geeta said it's like watching a fitness video but not doing the workout. In that context, it seems completely ridiculous. However, that is exactly what we are doing with business. We gather all this info but never fully put it into action and then accuse it of not working. This circles back to understanding you and how you think. This keeps most people on the quest for new ideas forever, with little implementation. If you don't implement, you don't gain sustainable momentum. When you can connect the implementation with the knowledge, acceleration happens.

In my interview with her, Geeta said we have a battle going on between our conscious and unconscious minds. Our conscious mind helps make the decisions you are most familiar with. Your unconscious mind helps you control your breathing, your heart beating, or even growing a baby. For me, my conscious mind wanted to charge more, stay firm on pricing, and make swift decisions, but my unconscious mind was rejecting it. Much of this was programmed during my childhood. Most of what our body does typically defaults to our unconscious mind. Until I was able to connect the two, my unconscious mind was sabotaging what I wanted from my conscious mind. In other words, typically what is programmed in your unconscious mind will always win. It will guide your decision making and how you lead, and it will influence all you do. If you do not create alignment with your unconscious and conscious mind, you will not achieve momentum. Understanding this battle and how to create alignment is the beginning of your journey to experiencing explosive momentum.

BECOMING AWARE OF LIMITING BELIEFS

I had had enough.

I was sitting in my office looking at numbers and was in denial. How could we lose $60,000 on one account? I was at a breaking point. I was angry. I was sick of the roller coaster, and I was ready for a change. The year was 2019. The years prior, I was in denial about how bad our numbers were. I made excuses about how we couldn't trust the data or how maybe there were errors in the paperwork. In 2016, we went digital, and by 2019, we had a robust database of service rates. It couldn't be denied anymore. We were flowing in two-year waves. In 2014, we had a massive sales year followed by massive challenges. We repeated this exact pattern in 2016 and 2018. One year of high, the next year of low. I now call this the crazy cycle.

I didn't realize at the time how my limiting beliefs were causing this to happen and affecting my whole organization.

During my childhood, we were extremely poor. I can still taste the exact flavor of Aldi hotdogs. Hotdogs were a regular food in our house because they were cheap. If they weren't in a bun, they were in soup or some other concoction my mom would create. We were blessed we weren't hungry, so I am thankful for having food. During my childhood, everything we did was based around the cheapest. My family looked for the best deal and never purchased anything of value. I never saw value or understood why someone would ever want it. Cheap always seemed to work growing up. I never knew anything different. This was forming the narrative in my subconscious that would haunt me for years in business, until I discovered it became my own limiting belief. A limiting belief is something you believe to be true that limits you in some way. The limiting belief could be about you, other people, or the world.[5]

I remember countless calls with my mentor, Dan. "What's going on? I just can't figure it out," I would say. He continued to question my pricing and if I was really selling value or price. I swore to him for over five years I was selling premium value, but my financial statements said differently. I realized on doing a deep dive into my mindset that I didn't really believe we could sell premium, and I didn't believe my company delivered premium service.

It still stings to write those words, but it was true. I knew we weren't, which led me to make decisions based on this subconscious belief. Let me paint a picture of how this played out and the impact it had.

1. 20 percent conscious self is confident. This attracts clients.

2. Our staff puts together customer estimates. Seth says, "That's too high; they won't pay that." Managers lower the price to what we think they'll pay.

---

5   Jane Taylor, "What Are Your Biggest Limiting Beliefs?" *Jane's Journal* (blog). accessed March 16,2020.

3. We win the job.

4. We buy a lot of equipment.

5. We have a payment on new equipment to service a new job that we are losing money on.

6. We have high staffing needs because of rapid growth. We end up hiring anyone with no training. They deliver poor service.

7. Employees get hurt or do damage to property because we didn't train them well, so our insurance rates go up, costing more money.

8. Because we didn't screen them, the new employees quit after two weeks, so our unemployment rates skyrocket.

9. Everyone is maxed out because of complaints, and if we say anything to our staff, they'll quit, so we need them to work so we get paid.

10. We don't enforce quality.

11. We lose the account.

12. We repeat this and accept more bad accounts, because we need something.

13. Crazy cycle starts for next year.

Anyone who reads that can 1,000 percent see that is a dumb plan, but why couldn't I? I knew it wasn't good, but I wasn't strong enough to change it until I saw it clearly. Having this limiting belief was costing my company a lot of money, friction, and wasted energy.

During my initial call with Geeta and her team, I tried to negotiate their price, and they asked me one of the most powerful questions that cemented premium into my head.

She said, "Seth, you do realize you are your customer?" I paused. She knew she got me. She continued, "You know you attract the customer who you are. If you always have to think about it when you are working with a customer, you will attract the same."

That hit me hard. All these years I was looking for low-cost providers, and I ended up attracting low-margin work. I realized at that moment that I was aligned this way, and until I broke free from this way of thinking, I would never get ahead.

This new awareness, combined with the correct mindset, has led to explosive healthy growth in all of my businesses in a short time. Perfect, no. Once I got the foundation correct, everything fell into place and became easier. I share this because I want you to experience the same!

You have limiting beliefs holding you back from your greatest you. Now is the time to unlock them.

MY JOURNEY TO START THE MO

I had recently completed my Executive MBA at Villanova in the spring of 2019 and was testing the market to see what was out there. My favorite part of what I do is coaching people. It has become my passion to help others succeed. I also had just spent $100,000 on an MBA. As a business guy, I was putting pressure on myself to get a return on my investment.

My initial thought was to work for a global firm and do consulting in human capital, with future of work focus, with one of the big four consulting firms. I always felt that my companies were able to adapt ahead of the times regardless of the situation. The future of work, according to Deloitte is "the growing adoption of artificial intelligence in the workplace, and the expansion of the workforce to include both on- and off-balance-sheet talent." In layman's terms, this is figuring out how we blend people with technology. One of the biggest myths is that people will be replaced. In reality, people will blend with technology in the future. At this point, I was targeting Deloitte, McKinsey, BCG, and Accenture. I did have many conversations with recruiters, principals, and even the CEO of Deloitte, Cathy Engelbert, who is now the WNBA commissioner. Nothing was clicking at that point.

I remember connecting with Deloitte partner Jason Reilly after a golf tournament at Hershey Country Club. I was sharing with him my passion for helping people, and he pointed out that my focus was not narrow enough. He sent me the 2019 Deloitte Future of Work Report and suggested that I read it to understand what was going on and where I could fit in. I went home and read the whole report. I dialed in more on the future of work, however, I was still lost. You see, I have never navigated the corporate job space. If I had to sign a corporate deal, no problem, but this was new territory.

I felt like a college kid who had just graduated and was looking for a job. It was overwhelming. Up to this point, I had been a serial entrepreneur. I had never been paid by another organization in my adult life except for the ones I started. Jason Reilly was onto something that day on the golf course, but it didn't click right away. After being extremely frustrated, I decided to do what I do best: start my own momentum.

I looked over many business topics as I looked to develop my own coaching program. When I searched for leadership, John Maxwell popped up. When I searched business coaching, Tony Robbins and Brian Tracey appeared. Grant Cardone was trying to 10X everything, and Dave Ramsey was trying to save everything. I realized in that moment no one owned the topic of momentum. Momentum was a force everyone had experienced, and all of the above had components of momentum, but I was seeking to break down how to get it and how to keep it.

I was so excited that I was ready to inject momentum in any way possible. However, I was still lost on focus and clarity. According to my plan, I was going to be an interim executive; in between that job, I would do keynote speaking and coach executives on the side. If that wasn't confusing enough, I advertised that I was an investor and entrepreneur. I remember being with a group of executives in the suites at the Wells Fargo Center watching a basketball game. After I shared all my roles, I remember another executive asked, "What do you do? How do you do it?" At this point, I did not know.

I was lost with no direction. That is when I had my epiphany call with Geeta.

THE EPIPHANY CALL AND THE
EPITOME OF AWARENESS

I felt like I was lying there exposed after my epiphany call.

Geeta was right. Right about everything. I remember being on the phone with her and it felt like she was reading right through me. She had been there. This was my future coach, Geeta Nadkarni.

A few weeks before our call, her advertisements kept popping up on my social media platforms. To be honest, I'm not sure how I was targeted, but somehow I was. I have viewed two online webinars in my life from ads. One was with Geeta Nadkarni and the other was a public speaking training with Brian Tracey. All the other ads passed through my feed without a second glance. On this day, I clicked on Geeta's advertisement, and I felt like she was talking to my inner soul. I felt as if she knew me and what I wanted. But how could that be, when *I* didn't even know what I wanted?

That call opened my eyes, created awareness to my blind spots, and accelerated my momentum to my now popular, high-ticket coaching program, Momentum U. Through Momentum U and my seven steps, I help business owners and coaches:

U—Understand limiting beliefs

N—Dive deep, creating true value

L—Learn to amplify, connect, and close

O—Operate with lower costs

C—Connect better with team and customers

K—Kill it! Increase profit by 5–10 percent

When you do the above, it results in more net profit. Not only does our program help business owners be profitable, but it also helps them become balanced in their lives again.

HUMBLE BEGINNINGS

It was a perfect eighty-degree day in early June. I had just completed my permit requirements for my driver's license. Instead of taking off for the beach or a concert, I had a few clients lined up to do yard work. When you start a lawn business as a kid, typically you take on any work you can get, and most times it's not glamorous—more like brush clearing or hard manual labor jobs. I'm not sure which was less glamorous, the work I was doing or the 1993 Ford Tempo car with a gutted pop-up camper that I used as my trailer to pull our family Snapper lawnmower. I was officially the laughingstock of the town, but I didn't know. I was on a mission.

As I parked and stepped out of my car, my stepdad came out with a verbal assault. "You never take care of anything. You are never going to use the mower again." This was not the first time I dealt with verbal abuse from him. I was done with this.

That was the day I left home forever. I was sixteen years old.

Looking back, it was the exact moment where my momentum started. I'm not sure I calculated the ROI of this decision, but it proved to be one of the best in my life. I have found that starting true momentum typically begins with the most difficult decisions. Most times, difficult decisions cause discomfort; however, I have found that the harder the decision is, the more momentum you stand to gain. I faced the world at an early age and failed miserably along the way, but that is why I continue to succeed.

FINAL THOUGHTS

Awareness and mindset are the foundation of momentum. Once you understand this, you will be able to unlock the momentum that you have been dreaming of in your business and life. Do not underestimate their power. Mindset is a superpower when you dive deeper to understand how it works. It allows you to identify limiting beliefs and blind spots.

Limiting beliefs are a thief of your true potential and are seldom recognized. When they are exposed and understood, you will be able to make better decisions in your life and business because you have now taken off the brakes. Blind spots are areas that you cannot see yourself. If you are not aware of them, you cannot improve. We all have them. The best way to uncover them is to have another perspective, which will help you grow.

If you are starting a new business, you will be able to grow much quicker if you understand mindset and awareness. If you are an existing business and you continue to wonder why everything you try is only working for a short period of time, I guarantee the root cause is awareness and mindset. When you do a deep dive into the root of your thinking, everything you learned over the years will suddenly have a new lens, and you will understand how to use it to sustain momentum. When mindset meets strategy, it creates explosive momentum.

CHAPTER 2

THE HIDDEN VALUE

———

"We tend to overvalue the things we can measure and undervalue the things we cannot."

—JOHN HAYES

I uncovered over 1.2 million dollars in less than eight weeks with my first Momentum U client. I knew I was onto something.

MY FIRST MOMENTUM U CLIENT

John had no idea that his business was dying from hidden costs. John owned a painting business but had been in corporate America in human resources and insurance benefits for most of his life. In the corporate world, he understood the importance of hiring the right talent and providing a positive culture. He even had his interview questions perfected so candidates would be more vulnerable in their answers and show their more authentic side.

However, even with his corporate success, he decided to cash in his retirement to have a part of the American dream: the dream of owning a business, being an entrepreneur, and being his own boss. When I asked John why he did this, he said, "I saw it as a great opportunity to help people. I chose a CertaPro franchise because of the support and training for my staff. Out of all the franchises, they did the most for their people."

The hype wore off quickly, and the hard truths of owning a business started to show up. Finding good help, managing cash flow, and wanting to control every aspect of his business were just a few challenges he faced. After four years of being a business owner, he had not witnessed a profit. John began losing faith in the American dream.

"I put everything I had into my business at the expense of my family life, health, and retirement." On top of this, he had not been on a vacation in the last three years. That was the year I met John. For John, he didn't have a choice. He had to win this year. We briefly talked about the alternative, but we were both committed to his success. I knew I could help John, and I love it when the pressure is on.

One of my strengths as a coach is to identify the problem quickly with my Momentum U team. In working with John, my team and I recognized his intense desire to help others—so substantial that he neglected what he needed most.

Society praises selfless acts and putting others first, which is good to a point. When a person thinks they have something to give, but in reality they do not, it can cause more challenges. In John's case, he was not making money, but he was giving to others, further draining himself. Identifying this led to help change John's business and life forever.

The transformation started on our initial call when I listened to John blame his sales rep and admin over and over again. I'm not sure he realized how much he was doing it, but as a coach, I listen and take notes. I finally said, "Who hired them? Why are you keeping them? Why did you hire them?"

John begrudgingly said, "I did. I'm not sure why I'm keeping them." The next answer to my question about why he hired them unlocked his future transformation.

He said, "They were in a bad spot and needed help."

Bingo! On the first call, I was on to something.

John could feel something was different, and he committed to Momentum U. My two amazing mindset coaches, Nikki and Taylor, joined in on the first call. We helped John understand that during his four years in business, he was making all of his decisions through the lens of helping people, not hiring the best person. Imagine this: a person who is drowning and cannot swim is trying to save another person who is drowning. The outcome is most likely two casualties.

John is a perfect example of someone not understanding the hidden costs of their thinking. Helping people was making him feel good but ultimately making him feel worse because he really had nothing to help with. This way of thinking was leading to hiring very poor staff, which in turn led to low-quality work, upset customers, and the feeling that John had to do more to control the situation. At the end of the day, the biggest place it was showing up was with stress and the lack of money in his bank account. One step farther. Stress and lack of money put a strain on relationships and quality of life.

AWARENESS INTO ACTION

John was now aware that his desire to help people—before he had the ability to help himself—was hurting him the most. Even after discovery, the real journey happens when awareness turns into action. Action is hard.

I remember getting an email from John after we uncovered his barrier to success. He explained how he connected with a family on a sales call, and because of their story, he did their job for his cost. John fell back into his old ways and did not even realize it. As a coach, I'm going to be the bad guy here for a minute. I know you are thinking that is great and John is an outstanding person for helping. The hidden impact is that he did not have that to give. If you recall from earlier, I stated that he had not made a profit since he started his business. If I shared all of the challenges that John was facing in his business, you would agree that he needed the money more than this family. The hidden cost of helping others was wearing John down and leaving nothing for him.

One day on our call, I finally asked him, "Are these people much better off after you 'helped' them?"

I was expecting a firm yes.

He delayed and said, "Not really. They are basically the same."

I asked, "Why do it then?"

He was beginning to see how this hidden cost was eroding his profits year after year, and, until this point in time, he had no idea. To clarify, after you make money, if you want to give it all away to charity and to help the world, that is your choice. As a coach, I'm going to help you make money, so you can decide how and what you want to do with it.

Just like John's example, awareness can come early and lead to fast action if you are open to it and coachable. You do not always see the hidden costs. Once we understand the issue, we can begin to overcome what has been holding you back.

HIDDEN COSTS AND BLEEDING MONEY

"That's way too much money!"

This was my response after I saw what was drafted from my account for unemployment. How could this be?

My commercial service business was bleeding money because I was looking at the wrong information. It was hidden. In fall 2018, we had a sales explosion. We increased operations, bought trucks and equipment, and made sure we were set up and ready to go. It was easy to figure out based on our metrics how many trucks or how much equipment would be needed to deliver the service. The next part was adding staff. I would estimate we talked to over five hundred people through career fairs, online ads, reaching out, and referrals. The problem was when spring hit, we didn't have enough people, so we threw out everything we knew about taking our time in interviewing to just look for anyone who would show up. As you can imagine, the challenges were immense. I remember thinking I would not want any of these people on my property.

We forfeited experience
↓
Thought we could train them

Didn't drug test
↓
Opened the door to problems

Didn't check references
↓
Stories weren't verified

Tolerated late and call-offs
↓
Made dedicated people mad—led to inconsistent work.

Frustrated my staff
↓
Affected culture and positivity

These were just a few of the challenges we faced. Even as I write it out, I'm embarrassed at how I could allow this to happen. If we would have calculated the monetary cost to these areas, as if the headaches weren't enough, we would have never gone this way. The sad part is we were getting ready to continue this biannual cycle until I saw the draft of funds the following season. We had hired over fifty people and many of them did not work out. It was my fault for allowing this. Our unemployment percentage was through the roof because of all the hires and fires. Only then did I realize the cost and start to tie everything together. I saw the money leaving, and it hit me.

I remember finally connecting all the dots to realize the hidden cost of these decisions was leeching our business of money. We thought we were strong and working through all the other challenges. We were good firefighters. When I read the above, it still slaps me in the face. How could I not see the impact?

I have learned that we must convert our challenges into clear dollar amount costs. We understand money. When a business owner looks at their financial statement, the impact of poor decisions shows up in their net profit; however, these are difficult to identify. It is essential to put a monetary value on these non-financial statement areas to see what is costing you most. In the above example, we saw the cost throughout our organization.

Once we connected the dots of impact, we were able to identify the root of our problem. We found that our sales target was wrong. We found that by selling large-scale properties, fifty-plus-acre properties, they were an easy sell, a low-profit margin, demanded additional labor, and were a strain on cash. By identifying this hidden cost, we were able to pivot to targeting high-profiting, smaller clients who needed less staff to service, eliminating our problem while reducing our rates. We also had to have tough conversations with clients who were no longer a fit. Once we understood the impact, in dollars, we were able to confidently raise our prices and know that if it didn't work for them, it was in the best interest of our total organization. These costs were hidden from us until we put a value on it—then we fixed it. You can too.

HIDDEN COSTS—DETERMINING THE MONETARY VALUE

In today's world, we track everything except what matters most. The most substantial value is often hidden in what we do not track, and that is where many companies are losing the most money. They continue to look at the numbers they measure and neglect to put a value on what I call the non-balance sheet costs.

First, let's look at how Value and Return on Investment (ROI) are defined.

Value:

1. the monetary worth of something [6]

2. something (such as a principle or quality) intrinsically valuable or desirable sought material *values* instead of human *values*—W. H. Jones

3. a numerical quantity that is assigned or determined by calculation or measurement.

---

6   *Merriam-Webster*, s.v. "value (*n.*)," accessed March 18, 2020.

Return on Investment (ROI) is a performance measure used to evaluate the efficiency of an investment or compare the efficiency of a number of different investments. ROI tries to directly measure the amount of return on a particular investment, relative to the investment's cost [7]

I share multiple definitions because they all apply to how we look at value. First, it has monetary worth. However, in business, it is not always something you can sell and recover a fee. The second definition by *Merriam-Webster* is a principle or quality. For example, if you have an employee who stole money from you, you understand that employee is not a valuable asset to your company, but we don't often consider the inverse: the value of having a company made of honest people. Honest people mean your company will function more fluidly and efficiently.

As a coach, I have found most people struggle to assign value if it is not monetary. The more we understand value and ROI prior to making decisions, the less it will cost us in the future. In the dishonest employee example, understanding the value of a trustworthy person and investing more in the hiring process has significant value and return. The inverse would be looking at the cost of a dishonest employee. Either way, there is a clear number that can be put on the situation.

The third *Merriam-Webster* definition combines the first two by putting a numerical quantity, most times money, that we can assess and connect to understand.

---

7   *Entrepreneur Encyclopedia*, s.v. "Return on investment," Entrepreneur Media, accessed March 18, 2020.

For most people, having a definite cost associated with an account is what 95 percent of all decisions are based on. Most businesses rely heavily on their P&L (Profit and Loss) and their Balance Sheet, which are both financial statements. However, the P&L and Balance Sheet do not evaluate the cost and benefit of employee retention, the cost of a disengaged employee, or the power of a supportive work culture. That is why we should look so hard at what I call "off-balance-sheet costs."

Many times, these categories have more of a financial impact than the categories we regularly review. For example, the stock market. The S&P 500 gauges the performance of the stocks of the five hundred largest, most stable companies in the New York Stock Exchange—it's often considered the most accurate measure of the stock market as a whole and is a number that businesses review regularly. They want to see their return from their ROI. The current average annual return from 1923 (the year of the S&P's inception) through 2016 is 12.25 percent.[8] If you want a much higher return in your organization, evaluate hidden costs. You will find excess money when you look. Most times, organizations are looking at the wrong information.

THE HIDDEN COST OF CHARGING FEES

The hidden cost of the late fee helped bring down Blockbuster.

Blockbuster, a movie rental store had nine thousand stores globally and a revenue of 5.9 billion, which peaked in 2004.[9]

---

8   "Return on Investment; the 12% Reality," RAMSEY, accessed March 18, 2020.

9   Frank Olito, "The Rise and Fall of Blockbuster," *Business Insider*, August 20, 2020.

At the time, it made 16 percent of its revenue from late fees from its customers. It was viewed as an untouchable powerhouse. What was it missing? A significant part of its revenue was based on negative interactions with its customers. Yes, it was the customers' fault if they did not return the movie on time. Regardless, the interaction is negative. Customers would make excuses to avoid costs and never return because they had late fees, which in turn stopped them from renting more. This became a recipe for disaster and a hidden cost that provided an opportunity for another company to capitalize.

Netflix was that company. In 1997, Netflix started. It had a simple premise: remove all late fees. You were able to keep your movie as long as you wanted; however, you were not able to rent a new one until the old one was returned. Brilliant! This allowed the customer to feel like they were in control. In 2019, Netflix generated $20.15 billion and had a valuation of $239 billion.[10] Blockbuster focused on the $1 billion in profit they had from late fees. Where the disconnect happens is when an organization sees $1 billion in revenue on its financial statements but does not realize the hidden cost of that activity is much more costly. Building on what we know so far about building momentum, Netflix started with the awareness by seeing the problem as well as the opportunity. It then calculated the value of doing business differently, and it has led to incredible momentum. In 2020, Netflix was valued at $239 billion.[11]

10   "Netflix Revenue 2006-2020," Macrotrends, accessed March 25, 2020.

11   "NasdaqGS - NasdaqGS Real Time Price," Netflix, Inc. (NFLX), accessed March 25, 2020.

THE HIDDEN VALUE OF MENTORSHIP

We fail to put values on areas of most impact because we don't know how. The numbers below represent the clear value of your investment in percentages. Most people look here, but the return is much greater if we look beyond the concrete numbers. These are concrete numbers that can't be disputed. They are facts.

From 1987 to 2016, the S&P's average was 11.66 percent.

In 2014, the market's annual return was 13.69 percent

In 2015, it was 1.38 percent.

In 2016, it was 11.96.[12]

As a five-year-old kid, I would look out the window at our house and see massive tractors take up the whole lane as they drove by. I loved equipment. My grandfather, Herman, who was my first "mentor" allowed me to run his equipment at an early age. I started on the lawnmower at five, and by seven, I was operating his Ford red belly farm tractor to mow his field. I was a tall kid, so at an early age, I could reach the pedals. By the time I was twelve, I was running lawn tractors and farm equipment proficiently and sought out whoever owned these "big tractors."

One of our neighbors knew the farmer and provided me their number. I was so excited. I remember calling on our landline phone. A man answered, Gern Sr., who at the time

---

12   "Return on Investment; the 12% Reality," RAMSEY, accessed March 25,2020.

was running the farm. "Hi, I'm Seth Lewis. I'd like to work for you and drive the tractors."

He asked, "How old are you? Do you have a driver's license?"

I responded, "No, I'm twelve, but I can run all the equipment. I run my grandpa's tractor."

He offered for me to help clean chicken houses, which I declined, but he said when I had a driver's license to call him back. As I continued to see the tractors drive by for the next couple of years, I remembered our conversation.

It was a summer day, and I was sixteen and working on my own. I was at another local farmer's place picking up some supplies when I met Gern Haldeman Jr., who was the son of Gern Sr., whom I spoke to on the phone years ago. He was now running the farm. At the time, I only had a few clients, so my work was pretty inconsistent. I offered to help. A couple of days later, I got a call to meet in a field around 1:30 p.m. I went and the rest is history.

I helped Haldeman Farms out for a couple of years while I was growing my landscape business. I would work a day or two doing my work and then work the remaining five or six with them. The best part was I got to meet some amazing people. During my time there I got to know Gern Jr., who helped provide me guidance. Since I was on my own and did not have a father in my life, he took me under his wing.

I remember being in his shop one day after I bought my first commercial mower from him and he said, "It's time for you to get a new trailer. You have to protect your investment. What you have is not safe and will end up costing you more especially if something happens."

I went out and bought a new trailer. I trusted him and I called him for advice many times over the years. When I've called, he's always answered and been there for me. There were many times I was wrong or was off course, and he was able to point it out in a way that helped me grow and learn as a person.

Mentorship is an excellent example of a hidden value. According to an analysis conducted by Endeavor, a nonprofit organization that supports high-impact entrepreneurs across the world, companies whose founders have been mentored by a top-performing entrepreneur are three times more likely to go on to become top performers themselves.[13] According to Inc.com, 70 percent of mentored businesses survive more than five years, double the rate for non-mentored small businesses over that same period.[14] Mentorship will not show up on a financial statement directly; however, the impact of having a great mentor has a strong correlation to the success of an organization. When you evaluate the impact of mentorship, I would argue that an individual would be foolish to not invest in a mentor-mentee relationship.

What is the return of having a mentor who helps guide your success? Is it higher than the S&P thirty-year average of 12.25 percent? I point this out because this is an investment that

---

13   Rhett Morris, "Mentors Are the Secret Weapons of Successful Startups," *TechCrunch*, March 22, 2015.

14   John Rampton, "How a Mentor Can Increase the Success of Your Business," *Inc.*, October 1, 2020.

people are happy with, but compared to the impact of mentorship, it is poor.

Even the highest-profile executives and owners have had mentors to guide their paths. Steve Jobs, founder of Apple, had Ed Woolard and John Sculley. Bob Iger, CEO of Disney, had guidance from Tom Murphy, who was his former boss. Bill Gates, founder of Microsoft, considers Warren Buffet a mentor of his.

Russ Klein, CEO of the American Marketing Association expressed his thoughts on the value of mentorship. "I've never gotten anywhere without other people along the way. Anyone who says they have… I think is maybe being economical with the truth. We all get along with the support and help of other people. When you can connect to a mentor who is both interested and dialed into what makes you tick… it's just so valuable and a gift."[15]

THE HIDDEN VALUE OF LOSING

The competition was being held at the Penn Stater Conference Center and sponsored by PNLA (Pennsylvania Nursery and Landscape Association), which also had a conference in conjunction. This was a way for industry leaders to learn more about current hot topics and trends and also get exposure to the best and brightest students.

The competition was set up such that students were acting as business owners, and they were meeting with a banker

---

15   "AMA CEO Russ Klein Talks about the Gift of Mentorship," AMA Toronto, October 10, 2019, video, 1:03.

to secure a line of credit. A line of credit is a pre-approved amount that a business can borrow from a bank without having to apply each time they need money for cash flow purposes. It is not for buying new equipment or assets; however, it helps with the natural cash flow. Cash flow tends to be up and down in any business. I had somewhat of an unfair advantage as I already had a business line of credit and met with my bankers on a regular basis. As I met with the "banker," I had the approval in a few minutes. I was able to demonstrate my knowledge of how lines of credit work and was able to pull the key info from the case to leverage it in my favor. I felt like I developed such a great rapport in those ten minutes that we continued to talk after I secured the loan.

I felt like I was the winner… I crushed it. It was one of those feelings when you know you've won almost right after you start something. I was making small talk with the business owner who was playing a banker, feeling the win. I could tell from the facial reactions of the judge. During the competition, he was trying to hold back that kind of smile when you know someone is mastering the questions asked. He continued to try and stump me with questions and for each, I flawlessly navigated, like a skilled surgeon's hands on a crucial operating procedure. I did not know at the time that the next thirty seconds would change my life forever. As the timer went off, I realized that I had not shaken the hand of the banker to finalize or "close the deal." This was a requirement that I had missed and was the final step to signal the pitch was complete. At that moment, I realized this mistake might cost me the competition.

As they announced the winners of the event, it was not me. I thought I knew why, but I wanted to be sure. I always want to know how to improve. As everyone was walking to lunch, I found the "banker" judge and asked him, "Why didn't I win? What could I have done differently?"

Asking this question made a big impression on the judge. Here was a kid who didn't take losing as an option. For me, it was not over after I lost—it was only the starting point of finding out how to win! We proceeded to go to lunch and talk. I learned that he was actually a leader in the industry, and we connected. I'm sure the initial impression that was made was him seeing if I would be a fit in his organization to hire me after graduation. In any event, there is always an opportunity.

As I moved forward from that moment, my relationship with Dan, the banker from the competition, grew. It grew naturally, and Dan turned into a business mentor who changed my life. Dan helped me with business challenges and supported me during the times I made rookie business mistakes, like not understanding my financial statements, cash flow, or how to lead people. His support was unwavering when I didn't deserve it.

A mentor relationship can be formed in many ways, but when it is organic, it has the most power. "A great mentor is someone who offers objective advice, provides counsel from a fresh perspective, is willing to collaborate, listen, and learn, as well as helping you stay focused on your goals, your purpose, and what you're working so hard to achieve," notes Amy Zimmerman, Head of People Operations at Kabbage.[16]

---

16   Kate Harrison, "New Study Reveals Entrepreneurs Need More Mentoring," *Forbes*, October 30, 2018.

According to *Forbes*, 76 percent of people think mentors are important, but just 37 percent have a mentor.[17] The value or return of having a mentor is priceless. I know I would be out of business currently if I did not have a mentor to help guide me. To see how that would impact me monetarily, let's look at an example. Let's use $1 million per year. I'll let you determine if that's your gross sales or your net profit. Either way, over ten years, that is $10 million. If you work forty years, that is $40 million. For me, without Dan and Gern, I would have lost the opportunity to be in business. This concept demonstrates a significant value that is important in the business process. This has an impact not only in your business or organization but on all the people and families who are connected to your organization. I would argue the number is larger because of the impact you will have on other people, your staff, their families, and the community. The impact multiplies many times.

My goal when I talk about ROI is to give business owners a different perspective of what may have significant value for their business but may be under the radar. If I have a $40 million asset on my team, a mentor, and you don't, who is going to win the end game? Who is more likely to have success? If you knew a mentor was worth $40 million, would you want one in your life and your business?

---

17 Christine Comaford, "76% of People Think Mentors Are Important, but Only 37% Have One," *Forbes*, July 3, 2019.

THE HIDDEN VALUE OF EMPLOYEE ENGAGEMENT

Employee engagement and customer retention is another key indicator of ROI, but the true cost or benefit does not show on the current balance sheets. Many businesses continue to analyze their numbers but overlook the costliest part of their business! A disengaged employee costs 34 percent of their annual salary.[18] That means for every $50,000 you pay someone if they are not engaged, it could be costing you $17,000. If you have ten team members who are disengaged because of your culture, it could be costing you $170,000 or more. You do not have to be a CFO to look at the number and realize there is a problem. If that number were on your balance sheet, you would attack it with aggression and work until you got the number improved. However, because you can't clearly see it and define it, it continues to leech your success. It sucks out any momentum that you may get going.

If employee engagement or retention is not your issue, it's likely there is another one that is a silent killer. Everyone has an area that typically goes undetected and most times it's not showing on your financial statements. Because of this, it makes it hard for some owners to truly understand why they are not seeing their desired profit at the end of the year.

As I look back to that day when I lost in the sales competition, I won. I actually hit the lottery. I'm here today because of mentorship and what I have learned from it. The examples above helped my awareness and added value to my businesses that I could have never actually paid for to achieve the same result.

---

18 Karlyn Borysenko, "How Much Are Your Disengaged Employees Costing You?" *Forbes*, May 2, 2019.

As life happens, always know that losing sometimes creates the most value and the returns are the greatest in times of loss.

—SETH LEWIS

FINAL THOUGHTS

Hidden costs are underestimated and usually not considered prior to making company decisions. It is not always about having all the data, because that can slow your decision-making. It is important to have the most impactful data. Hidden costs can have more negative impacts than anything that directly shows up on your financial statements. Hidden costs will indirectly show up in your organization's profitability, but it's about going deeper to find the root cause and fix it instead of patching it. As you practice this concept, you will be able to see areas of impact and make decisions in a more holistic method.

Value is being able to define what you offer in a way that sets you apart from your competition. Most leaders that I work with think they are clear on the value they offer to their customers. It is only clear in their mind. Spending time to define your value so your customer understands it will increase sales because they will understand what you do or offer and allow you to offer premium services, all which increases overall company success.

CHAPTER 3

DEFINE YOUR VALUE

———

Products are made in the factory, but brands are created in the mind.

—WALTER LANDOR

Ninety-nine percent of the clients I work with cannot define their value. One hundred percent of them believe they can.

The same happened for Joe Foster, the founder of Reebok.

In the eighties, Reebok was the number one brand in the world, thanks to the founder, Joe Foster.

I asked Joe what life is like after leading a number one global brand. Retirement "is not hard; it's not easy. I have enjoyed driving through Europe, visiting the many friends and former Reebok distributors in France, Germany, Italy, and Greece, eventually seven years ago returning to Tenerife to make a start on my book." The book Joe was talking about is *Shoemaker*, published in October 2020, about the rise of the global brand, Reebok. Ironically, that is how Joe and I connected.

We were both working on our books. We shared some of the excitement as well as the hard work, many hours, countless edits, and rewrites it takes to write a good book. Through connecting, Joe shared some of his story.

Joe's grandfather, Joe Foster, started J W Foster & Sons as a shoemaker. He developed a reputation for high-quality shoes and developed the first spiked running shoe in 1895. "At age seventeen, I was to join J W Foster & Son's, which was now being run by my father Jim and Uncle Bill. At eighteen, I was conscripted to do national service for two years. In 1952, my brother and I returned to the family business and were appalled at the stagnation and the need to modernize—not just the machinery and techniques but their business methods. Jeff and I tried to get Father and Uncle to make the changes but by now they were feuding with each other. Our pleas fell on deaf ears, leaving us with no alternative but to set up our own company. Knowing what our grandfather achieved propelled our mission."

"We didn't want to compete with the J W Foster business, so we decided to sell cycling shoes and call our company Mercury Sports Footwear. It was a very small business, but we were doing okay. We were instructed to register our name. Our agent came back to inform us that Mercury was already registered, and we would need to choose another name. He told us to bring a dozen. I had a *Webster's American Dictionary* I had won during the war at an athletics event, so I started looking up words. I remember thumbing through this and coming across the word 'reebok,' a light gray south African gazelle, which in an English dictionary, the spelling is 'rhebok'—not the same attraction. I put this at the top of the list, went back to our agent, and said, 'Look, here's your names, we want this one.' Out of all the ones we gave him, Reebok was the only one that cleared.

"We started advertising in *Cycling Magazine*. Our workshop was in an old Brewery in Bury, and it was so old that when it rained, water came in. We didn't buy new machinery. I used to pick stuff up at sales. At the time when we were building our business, there were so many shoe companies going under— once a month I'd be going to the sale of a shoe company which had closed down so I could buy machinery, leather, and bits like that. At the time, Jeff and myself, plus a guy called David, made the shoes, and my mother-in-law was doing the sewing.

"It was still difficult for an unknown athlete's shoe company. When I would go to shops, I would be greeted politely but be told 'I have Adidas and Dunlop, why do I need Reebok?' I understood that it was my job to make him need Reebok. My lightbulb moment came when I was watching a race we were sponsoring. They were my customers, and I needed to find a way to get to them beyond advertising in *Athletics Weekly* magazine." Joe then decided to target the clubs and provide a 15 percent discount if they became an agent. This led to many agents eventually setting up specialist retailers. They now began to see the value in Reebok.

"From that point, I realized my strategy was to be marketing-driven rather than production driven. My strategy was not to be a shoemaker."

This strategy worked well as they entered the US market that had volume demand.

"I had been exhibiting in Chicago every year since 1965, looking for a distributor, and now running was booming; this was to give us the opportunity we had been looking for.

"It was in 1979 when I bumped into Paul Fireman in Chicago. Paul was a camping wholesaler; he sold fishing lines and anything to do with camping. He said, 'I'd love to distribute your shoes, but I really need to know we've got a winner. If you get a five-star rating in *Runner's World*, I'm in,' We got three five-star ratings and the Aztec was one.

"Kmart was also interested, they said, "Look, we'll take twenty-five thousand pairs. But you need to get the Aztec down to this price,' We were making one thousand pairs a week in Bury, so that'd be six months' work. We would have to change; we couldn't expand manufacturing to that sort of volume or meet the price in the UK.

"It would be impossible to work with Kmart without sourcing products from the Far East. Twenty-five thousand pairs was tempting, but it would take time. I had already been contacted by an agent for a factory in Korea, but it was still early days.

"So the decision was made to go with Paul Fireman, who eventually became our CEO. That's how we started in America."

Paul also is credited for the idea of using the union jack on the Reebok shoes.

"Joe, can we put the Union Jack on the shoe instead of the Starcrest? It's going to cost us millions to get people to recognize our logo, but everyone will recognize the Union Jack.

"So we put the Union Jack on the shoes and put them in a Union Jack box. In those early days, we didn't have any point-of-sale stands, so the retailers would stack boxes in their window and then put shoes on the top. It was incredible: all of a sudden the business went from $9 million, to $30 million, to $90 million to $300 million to $900 million in successive years.[19]

The momentum continued for Joe and Reebok. He credits his team and great people like Angel Martinez, who went on to become CEO of Decker's brands, which includes lines like UGG, for recognizing the importance of designing a shoe specifically for aerobics. "Angel Martinez had joined Reebok as a tech rep in California and was intrigued by the new 'aerobic fitness classes' his wife and her girlfriends were going to. He decided to go with her and check it out. He discovered it was a small but growing new way of exercising to music that women were enjoying with the added benefit of getting fit. What got his attention the most was the women's footwear or lack of it. Some were exercising in bare feet, others a mixture of running shoes or plimsolls. Angel saw the need to offer a shoe specifically for aerobics and specifically for women."

Throughout his career, Joe was surrounded by great people. He even reflected on the CEO after Paul Fireman tried to bring strict workplace regulations when Reebok culture was freer and encouraged creativity. Joe highlighted a few things in the end: Keep awareness and always be ready to change plans. Make plans well in advance but stay nimble. Know what

---

19   Sam Waller, "Interview: Joe Foster, Reebok Founder," *Oi Polloi* (blog), November 4, 2019.

influences the sales of your company, watch for or be prepared for changes in your market, and ensure you have good financial access to cope with the growth momentum brings!

Joe's retirement has been interrupted by history knocking on his door, such as the IRS in the United States seeking information that has required him and his team to fly to Washington, D.C. for a few days here and there—just many events for a global brand founder trying to wind down at eighty-five but still in the game. "Seems I could retire but not leave. It's not hard. It's not easy. It never is.

In August 2005, Adidas acquired Reebok as a subsidiary, uniting two of the largest sport outfitting companies but maintaining operations under separate brand names. Adidas acquired all of the outstanding Reebok shares and completed the deal valued at $3.8 billion.[20]

FINAL THOUGHTS

Reebok's momentum was due to its clearly defined value. I learned from Joe, and I want you to learn that he was turned down. He was turned down because he was not able to convey his value to the shops. Even though he knew the value and believed in it, the customer did not. As he went around to shops, they told him that they had Adidas and Dunlop. Until he was able to define his value and create value that the customer understood, Reebok was going nowhere. The best and most successful organizations become so crystal clear

---

20 "Sportswear Maker Adidas to Buy Reebok for US $3.8 billion," *The New York Times: International Business*, August 3, 2005.

on their value and message that their customer understands and is attracted to them. Throughout Joe's story, there were consistent countless examples in which he added value to his brand that the customer was willing to pay a premium for, which fueled his momentum. Adding the Union Jack box was another form of value that people associated with and wanted to be a part of. Some people bought his shoes because of the Union Jack box. In the aerobics example, his team understood what the customer needed before it was created. When they developed the product, the demand was strong. When organizations are able to dive deep into understanding their value, they bring a clarity that attracts their customers. When customers understand what an organization offers, it creates alignment and allows for high-ticket, premium offerings.

CHAPTER 4

CULTURE

Shaping your culture is more than half done when you hire your team.

—JESSICA HERRIN, FOUNDER STELLA & DOT

When I asked Jordan Norwood about momentum, his answer shocked me. Jordan Norwood is a Super Bowl-winning wide receiver. He played for the Denver Broncos in 2015 when they won the Super Bowl. What surprised me about his answer was he highlighted a high school basketball game that he was part of. In 2003, the State College High School basketball team was in the state playoffs, and it was going up against Chester High School. Chester High School, in Pennsylvania, is a basketball dynasty. It has more championships in basketball than most schools have in all sports combined. State College going up against Chester was like going up against a basketball Goliath.

Prior to getting to the championship game, State College kept winning games, and their confidence was building slowly but surely. They had games that were won at the buzzer and shots that were going in and felt destined to win a state title. They could feel the energy just building the momentum behind them. During the state championship game, they were staying close with Chester, and the longer the game went on, the more their confidence rose.

It all changed when their star player, Jordan's brother Gabe, fouled out with a minute left. The team rallied and the other players stepped up to close out the game and win the state title. The culture of support, family, and team was something that stuck with Jordan, and it was something he was able to come back to during his up-and-down professional career. If you ask Jordan where he felt momentum, this is the first spot he will recall. I highlight this moment of our conversation because many people think momentum only happens on a large scale. Here is someone who won the Super Bowl, and he felt it the most during a high school basketball season.

I want you to know that momentum is all around us. It's something that we can all experience at any level. It goes back to everyday life, moments that we experience without being on the "biggest stage."

MOMENTUM TO THE SUPER BOWL

Jordan has always been the underdog. Going into Penn State, he was 150 pounds. That is considered small for a Division 1 football player. He was always counted out as not being good enough. His NFL career began by being undrafted. He signed with the Browns, only to be cut by them a short time later. He jumped around among many teams. He was released, he was cut, and he was injured. But at the end of the day, he went out on top because of the slow momentum that built up over his NFL tenure. In 2014, he ended up signing with the Denver Broncos, which ultimately won the Super Bowl in 2015.

Jordan focused his energy and effort on his faith. "If I could put my faith in God's promise for my life and do the hard work, I knew I would end up where I was supposed to be." When he finally got the opportunity, he capitalized. Few make it to the NFL. Even fewer get to play, and only a very select few get the honor to play with a Hall of Fame player like Peyton Manning. From day one, he could tell this organization was different than any other. When I asked him about the culture on that team, he shared with me, "When I was in the huddle, I knew I could count on everyone else there. We all felt the same way. There was a trust bond that was created among that team that I never experienced on any other team."

When I asked him where that came from, he said it was from Peyton Manning. Peyton set the tone of the culture and what he wanted the team to be. Jordan expanded on it and said, "Peyton made sure that he invested in the players. We did fun things like we went out to dinner. We would chop it up, play games, and really get to know each other besides just being Xs and Os. This built trust, a culture."

He made sure to highlight they were one of the worst offenses in the NFL that year. "We struggled on offense and were carried by our defense—a defense that is credited to be one of the best in NFL history. When we got to the plays that mattered, we could count on the other guy in our huddle and they delivered."

The culture they built as a team allowed them to win the "must-win" plays. Without the culture they established as a team, they might not be Super Bowl champions. There were a lot of areas in the season that they lost. They lost consecutive games. They had challenges and injuries and personnel problems. But the organization was clearly focused on winning, and Jordan said that wasn't the case in all organizations. I thought that was remarkable and surprising because you think every organization's goal is to win the Super Bowl. Jordan made it clear that investing in the culture of their organization made the difference when it mattered most and ultimately put them on top to win the Super Bowl.

ALL YOU GOT

The bell rang at 2:30 p.m., and it was time to go to football practice after school. I went out to my car to get my practice gear, and it wasn't there. I forgot it at home. I could feel the pain already. The conditioning, weight training, or whatever other punishment would be inflicted because of my mistake. It was an honest mistake, but it didn't matter. I was new to the football team so that didn't help. It was my first year playing high school football. I dreaded the conversation with my coach, but I went into the coaches' office and told my head coach, Rob Klock, that I forgot my practice gear. "Go home and get it," he told me, so I did. The whole car ride, I was frustrated. I was mad at myself and irritated at the thought of what I'd have to do when I got back to practice.

When I got back to the school, I quickly changed and joined my team. As I approached Rob, I was expecting the worst. Instead, he said, "Get out there and give it all you have today."

I was shocked. I'll never forget that day and how hard I practiced. There was no conditioning or weight training that would have substituted the energy and effort I put forth that day, not only that day but the rest of the season. This is a moment that has stayed with me in life and in business on the importance of culture. Culture is set by the leader. In this case, Rob built a positive culture around the program. The players he had were harder on themselves, and he knew that his established culture would handle minor situations like this.

Often organizations try to overmanage their culture, which makes it inauthentic and negative. In business, there have been many times when someone has messed up and has expected harsh repercussions from me. Instead, I have taken Rob's approach and told them, "Give me your all for the week." The impact is way greater and positive when you have the right people on your team.

THE FIX ALL MYTH

I believe culture is viewed as the "fix it all" solution in today's business world, which creates challenges when it comes to creating momentum.

Culture has and will continue to be a hot topic in business. I define culture as the personality of a business. Having a positive culture is not necessary for a company to be successful. When I make this statement, people look shocked. Let's examine Amazon. Amazon is one of the most successful companies in the world but, according to Startups.com, many employees have labeled the work culture as, "bruising," "relentless," and "churn and burn." That doesn't sound fun to me; however, everyone flourishes in different work environments. Companies outside of Amazon deem such a culture unfit, but it's hard to argue with a $1 trillion company evaluation.[21] Even so, as evidenced in those Amazon company reviews, lots of people like to point to culture as the root of many of a company's problems.

It is important to understand the personality of your organization and work within its framework. Culture is not one size fits all. The simplest way to understand your culture and how people perceive it is to ask questions. Talk to your employees or team members.

Earlier, we explored the value of awareness. In order for a company culture to be successful, you as a leader have to be aware of the strengths, weaknesses, and blind spots of your organization. Once you know the problem areas, you have a decision to make. Is the problem a minor complaint, or is it something that is costing the organization a significant amount of money?

When you get culture right, in addition to understanding awareness/mindset and the ROI, you will continue to pick up additional momentum

My service company had a team member who was with our company for seven years. Prior to working with us, she worked at a small-town grocery store at the front end. She did not have any office skills when she joined our organization, but she had a can-do attitude and was teachable. Seven years later, she ran

---

21 John Swartz, "Amazon Is Officially Worth $1 Trillion, Joining Other Tech Titans," *MarketWatch*, February 4, 2020.

our office. One Thursday afternoon, she walked into my office and told me that she took a position with another company. At this point in my career, I'm not sure I'm ever truly surprised by anything. I have an attitude of working to make the best of everything as it unfolds. The first thing I asked was whether there was something that we could have done differently. I think it is so important to have an open conversation at all times, but especially at the end, when nothing is holding a person back. This should be their most open candid feedback as long as they are not angry about something.

She told me that she had another offer she could not refuse. I congratulated her, and I took some time to remind her of who she became while she was with us and how she grew as a person. I reminded her of what she learned during the journey, not only as an employee but as a person. As tears fell from her eyes, she said she loved everyone at our company: "You guys will always be my family."

The moment was special to me because, as leaders, we don't sign up for anyone to pat us on the back. Our job is to encourage others and make them the best they can be. I take great pride in this. I have always said my goal is to make someone better by the time they leave us than when they started with our company. It is the most fulfilling part of my job. What I mean by this is helping people improve while they work for our companies is what I love. That is why I got into business coaching. I love to see people succeed. When the employee confessed her love for our company, I knew I had done what makes me happiest professionally.

She continued to say she could stay longer than two weeks so we would not be put in a bad spot. She also told me she wanted to stay a part of the team and help out part-time. She knew our system, and that really helped us out. This represents the culture and personality of our business. Sometimes, the most telling signs come from your people. Always be aware of your employees.

I stopped into the office over the weekend, after her last day, which I frequently do. On the second floor, we had a big whiteboard on the wall, about the size of a kitchen table. That day, it was covered in black ink. It reminded me of a full-page advertisement athletes or celebrities take out in a newspaper to thank a city for all they gave them. She wrote an emotional thank-you to all of us, explaining how much of an impact that we had on her life and that to her we would always be a part of her family.

One part stood out to me:

"I have been taught so much in my seven years of being here that I will take with me. I have built amazing relationships with great people and made amazing memories. I'm not gone, I'm here forever. I have so much love for this company and I can't wait to see what amazing things are in store. This is my home, where I feel my best at… I believe in each and every one of you to take off with everything this year. I love you so much."

—TEAM MEMBER

I took a picture and still have it to this day. I shared it with my wife to let her know everything a business owner goes through because the success, in the end, is worth it.

ASK

In a TEDx talk, Karen Maeyens says, "Questions are a powerful tool. They are the key to unlock many doors. They are the key to people, ourselves, and to the world."[22]

The power of asking your team questions on a regular basis is important to get ongoing, accurate feedback.

I was doing a routine check-in with one of our managers, Brandon. "What is your least favorite part of your job? How can I make your job easier?" I asked. Removing blocks will help him succeed and enjoy his job. This manager was in charge of assigning techs to jobs. Once the schedule was together, he would have to put in specific job notes for each client based on the need of the customer and/or what materials/ equipment the tech would need to take. He told me entering the daily notes for service techs was an added step that most times he had to do at night after working a full day. Instead of being about ready to come home and rest, he and his wife would care for their kids, and then after they went to bed, he would have to dive back into work.

First, I was appreciative of his open feedback about what was not working for him. In addition to this, we took time to examine other areas where people may need help and came

---

22   TEDx UFM, "The Value of Asking Questions," November 2017, video, 9:35.

up with five tasks or roles that needed to be broken up or added to continue to drive success and momentum. We knew that we had staff looking to grow with more responsibility, which we translated into more money. Once we defined the five roles, we put them out to our team and interviewed. For us, this did a couple of things.

How it helped our company:

- Showed us which staff wanted more opportunity and were willing to take steps to grow

- Showed our commitment to the existing team by providing them the first opportunity.

- Improved the culture

How it helped our team members:

- Lessened their workload and put them where they desired

- Improved two-way communication between management and operations

- Allowed for growth and additional compensation

These simple examples help build our culture and the personality of our company. The more wins you create that include everyone, the stronger your culture will be.

THE "WIN TRIANGLE"

What I have found to be a guide over the years to build momentum with our culture and company is our "Win Triangle." When I consider the team member, the customer, and the company, it has fueled success. When making decisions, including these three viewpoints are essential. Let's look at how each of these plays a critical role in building momentum.

The first is the team member. If the team member wins, we know they have a better quality of life and improved productivity positively affecting the bottom line.

The second is the client. When the client wins, they are happy with your service or product. They stay with your company as a customer. Did you know it costs 25 percent or more to obtain a new customer rather than keep the one you have?[23] Imagine if your customer believed in you so much they provided referrals and recommended you to their friends. Word of mouth is a powerful advertising tool that can essentially lower the cost of doing business.

Third, the company has to win. The company wins by making money and being profitable.

If you envision a balanced triangle, this is what we call our Win Triangle. If any of these areas get out of balance, it is typically an indication that it won't work long term. We encourage all of our team to bring solutions or recommendations that already fit through this lens. If your team knows

---

23   Amy Gallo, "The Value of Keeping the Right Customers," *Harvard Business Review*, October 29, 2014.

how decisions are made and can bring a solution to the table already meeting the requirements, it really empowers them to bring quality ideas.

Let me dive a little deeper with an example. You are a print shop, and you have a machine that prints, and then your team manually hand-trims the items printed. On average, one person cuts themselves each month. You have not had any major incidents yet. A team member mentions a new machine comes out that will print faster as well as trim. If we look at this simple illustration through the Win Triangle, here is what we see:

1. Team Member—Is safe and can complete jobs faster

2. Customer—Gets orders quicker, is happy, and tells others

3. Company—Keeps team safe, avoids workers' compensation claims, and has the ability to do more jobs.

We understand the company will have to invest in the new equipment and each company will have to evaluate its own numbers, but the advantages should cover the cost over time even in this simple example.

On the reverse, envision a triangle that is out of balance. A customer may want something beyond their contract and the company will lose money. The team member may want something selfishly that does not benefit the customer or company, or the company may make decisions that do not take the clients or team members into consideration. The more out of balance the Win Triangle is, the more issues you will have in your organization.

CULTURE FOR THE KIDS

Alignment of purpose drives success in organizations.

Bill Simpson, the former CEO of Hershey Entertainment & Resorts, had record success during his time at the helm. They had five consecutive record years under his leadership and paid out a record dividend to the Milton Hershey School. Bill was the CEO of Hershey Entertainment & Resorts Company from 2013 to 2018. Prior to being the CEO, he started as the general manager at the Hershey Lodge in 1996, then in 2002 he became the VP of the entertainment group, then in 2010 the COO, and then in 2011 was added to the board of directors prior to becoming the CEO in 2013.

When I asked him the secret to his success, alignment and purpose were used throughout our conversation. During his over twenty-year tenure with the company, he focused on alignment of purpose as the driving force behind all of his strategies, but it wasn't always that way earlier in his career. Just like it is for any leader, discovering the true purpose of his organization was an evolution of not only the company but of his personal growth as a leader.

Before Bill became the CEO of Hershey Entertainment & Resorts, he had a journey that provided many of the pieces that would build his success later as a CEO, as he hopped around the country in the hospitality industry. After completing his degree at Appalachian State University in North Carolina in hotel-restaurant management, he joined Hyatt Corporation and moved throughout the country, working his way up from a trainee to head of housekeeping to the director of rooms at numerous properties. Throughout his journey, he worked at high-end hospitality such as Gaylord Hotel in Nashville and Colonial Williamsburg, and he became a general manager of a management company that focused on hotel acquisitions. The Houston-based company acquired a hotel for 18 million, and in about twenty months sold it for 22 million with Bill as the general manager.

When asked what the key to the success of this company was, Bill said, "We really worked to push rates and deliver on service. The property had all the bones but needed a shot of enthusiasm. We had an executive committee that was aligned with our purpose. Our team was assembled from leadership from all of our other properties, so I did not have to teach them. It accelerated our transformation."

After the hotel was sold, the new company brought in their own team, and Bill found himself out of work. Shortly before the job change, Bill contacted the search firm that was retained to fill an executive position at Williamsburg. The recruiter informed him they already had a finalist for Williamsburg. They shared with him that there was an opportunity at the Hershey Lodge & Convention Center.

Bill put in for the general manager role, got interviewed, and was selected. He recalled the interview process as the most intense interview that he ever went through in his life. It was three and a half hours and over 150 open-ended, thought-provoking questions. As a part of being in town, he and his wife were able to get a tour of Hershey and hear the story of Milton S. Hershey, the founder of Hershey and the Milton Hershey School. They fell in love with the area and felt an immediate alignment with Milton Hershey's vision of supporting the Milton Hershey School and the students from disadvantaged homes.

Ninety days into the new role, Bill was tasked with presenting a $32 million initiative to the board of directors. It got approved. In addition to his job as a general manager, he also became the project manager to make sure it was delivered quickly. Life, and the company numbers, were good. It was all a success.

Great leaders have an innate ability to sense when something is off or missing. Five years into his journey, he realized what was missing. Up to that point in time, no one, not a single company, had invested a dime into teaching anything about leadership. It wasn't a "Hershey problem," it was a universal problem. Bill said, "I knew how to hit the numbers. I knew how to hit the margin. I knew how to do those things, but when it came to team development and leadership, and really hitting our stride, I came to realize I didn't know how to lead a team. How could I get the most out of people? Most importantly, I had to learn how to let go and trust people in power and hold them accountable. There is no question about it. I was a micromanager. I was guilty of owning other people's processes."

Bill sought out a coach and mentor to help him develop. His mindset began to change because of self-awareness. He gained the ability to see where he was currently and align himself with where he wanted to be. This allowed Bill to continue to break through and rise to the top. Momentum always begins with alignment of awareness and mindset. If you are not aligned in both as a leader, it will be extremely difficult to lead an organization and drive momentum.

A few years later, the CEO called Bill into his office to let him know the VP of the park was soon to be retiring. "The CEO asked me to consider the role and to take a month to decide if I wanted the job. I decided to take the job." Bill admitted he doubted that more than twenty years in hospitality would translate into amusement park management. After reflecting for a month, he decided to take the role. "I made the decision to take the job and go to the park, because I knew if I saved the lodge, it was a matter of time before I would just need to do something else. Because, you know, I'm a term limits guy. I think that you can only be at the peak of your game in a row for five or six years. You come in, you set your agenda, you accomplish your agenda, or you modify your agenda. And then if you're not careful, you slip into maintenance mode. When I think about momentum, that's where you put your momentum at risk. Because you've got to be a driving force, you've got to be a source of inspiration. You've got to keep the pressure on all the time for excellence in continuous improvement."

The new role at the park started out poorly. Six months into it, Bill was stuck. "It was December 27, 2002, and I called my coach and I said, 'I need to have a meeting with you. I'm pretty sure I'm miserable. And I'm even more sure that people that I'm working with are miserable too.'"

The journey of becoming a leader is challenging. Bill's mentor and coach quickly pointed out he was being too tactical and not allowing others to do their part. Success wasn't about his lack of amusement background but about his leadership skills—skills that still needed to be refined. But he had the curiosity and willingness to push himself beyond his comfort zone to grow.

At that moment, a switch happened in Bill's professional career that put him on a fast track for success. At the time, the park did not have a formalized feedback system for guests; they were only relying on problem feedback. They started to analyze their process to determine what needed to change. This allowed them to make sure they spent their capital improvement dollars in line with what the customers wanted.

In 2010, Bill was promoted to COO. COO is the title given to the next CEO of the company. It allows them a year to prepare prior to becoming the CEO. During the annual strategic planning session for the next five years, Bill noticed that all the annual meeting talked about was updates such as "how many chairs the lodge was going to buy." He quickly realized this was not true strategic planning and vision. Upon reflecting on the company's values, he couldn't remember them all, which led him to ask what they were really about.

The organization surveyed the people and came up with four key values that still stand today.

1. Dedicated to Legacy of our Founder (Mr. Hershey)

2. Selfless Spirit of Service

3. Team Focus

4. Respectful of Others

The next question that arose was what its core purpose was. When you think about this, it is amazing that an organization that was founded in 1927 did not recognize its core purpose. How could this be? Why does it exist? What is it here for?

After additional research, Bill came across a piece that Jim Collins wrote about uncovering your purpose. Jim Collins is an American researcher, author, speaker, and consultant focused on the subjects of business management, company sustainability, and growth. One of his most famous books is *Good to Great*. Bill went on to explain how to ask the five whys. The five whys is a technique in Collins' book that uncovers purpose by asking five "why" questions for every answer.

Question #1 What do we do as an organization? *Deliver Hershey Branded experiences.*

Question #2. Why do we deliver Hershey Branded experiences? *To keep our clients happy.*

Question #3 Why do we want to keep our clients happy? *To make money.*

Question #4 Why do we want to make money? *So we can be successful.*

Question #5 What is success? Giving back and supporting the Milton Hershey School.

The answer to the fifth question became its purpose. It was for the legacy that Milton Hershey started for the kids of the school.

Alignment and clarity happened! Now it was time to build on this.

Hershey Entertainment had connected to the purpose of its organization. It was deep. It was beyond feelings or one customer or employee. It was continuing to fulfill the legacy of the school. As the new CEO, Bill made a commitment that all his decisions would take into account the impact on the school. It gave new passion and mission to the overall big picture and the "why" to the whole corporation.

In addition to getting clear on the overall purpose, Bill committed to investing in three clear areas. "First, I invested in growth, which focused on new projects and capital improvements. Second was maintenance—making sure that the existing assets were up to date, clean, and presentable to guests. The third was human capital—how to invest in the people to make them great." Alignment continued to build on the deep found purpose.

The team developed a course that everyone had to take over eighteen months. It trained them on the culture and purpose of Hershey Entertainment. The course consisted of learning about the values of the company, spending time at the school, and learning from *The 7 Habits of Highly Effective People.*

During the program, employees reached out to Bill to let him know that the program had changed their lives by teaching them lessons beyond their work skills. Bill's mentor, Mr. Kreider, changed his life and, as the CEO, Bill looked to change the lives of others.

According to a study on companies that are clear on their purpose, 58 percent of companies with a clearly articulated purpose achieved growth of more than 10 percent over the past three years, 85 percent of companies with clearly articulated purposes showed some growth overall, while 42 percent of companies without it showed negative growth.[24]

This clarity and alignment of purpose allowed Hershey Entertainment to have five record years with profitability and growth. Hershey Entertainment went from barely being profitable in 2012 to paying out the largest dividend to the school in history: that is momentum!

Over Bill's time at Hershey Entertainment, he enacted several principles of building momentum. Bill was precise with his vision and strategy, which built a culture that produced record profits. As Bill Gates said, "Most people overestimate what they can do in one year and underestimate what they can do in ten years." In Bill's case, it was five years and a whole lot of happy kids at the Milton Hershey School.

FINAL THOUGHTS

Culture is a part of a successful company, but it is not the only driving factor. Culture is not a one-size-fits-all recipe that can be seen in a company like Amazon that is successful but has a workplace culture that is not always positive. An extreme opposite example is Costco, which makes employees the center of its mission. James Sinegal, the founder and former

---

24 Paul Grossinger, "5 Fascinating Stats Show Purpose Transforming Work," *Inc.*, September 22, 2020.

CEO said seventy cents of every dollar spent by Costco goes to employee wages, and the company has a 7 percent turnover rate, compared to 60 to 70 percent at other retailers.[25]

Both Costco and Amazon are successful companies while both having completely different cultures. Incorporating regular feedback, asking questions, and aligning your recruits with the culture you desire will keep your company moving forward. Understand the value, impact, and costs of the culture you decide to implement. Be intentional.

25   Barbara Farfan, "Quotes from Costo Founder James Sinegal: Quotations on Long-Term Success from a Successful Retail Leader," The Balance Small Business, updated March 31, 2019.

CHAPTER 5

STRATEGY

"Fitting in is a short-term strategy, standing out pays off in the long run."

—SETH GODIN

Have you ever been told your strategy sucks?

I remember the feeling after one of my coaching calls. She ripped me apart. In my head, it was perfect. It was going to work and work very well according to my vision, until I had someone rip it apart. I could see all the money flowing in, in my head, but when someone else heard my plan, it was laughable. As I shared prior, I was planning to be a public speaker, executive coach, interim executive, and help start-up entrepreneurs. I wasn't getting the hint when I went to business functions and people would ask me, "But what do you do?" Translation: You make no sense, dude!

My coach pointed out I lacked clarity in my offer. First, I didn't have a client, and even if I did have someone interested, they would have no idea how to buy from me. Let me point out one more obvious point. If your customer does not know how to buy, how you are different, or exactly what you sell, you will struggle in sales.

Within eight weeks of working with my coach, she helped me find clarity around my strategy, and I was making money. Not only was I making money, but I also shifted my thinking and strategy to be premium and high ticket, which changed everything.

STRATEGY THAT'S BLIND

One of my closest friends Shane shared with me he was starting a coaching business. He went through Dave Ramsey's Financial Peace program, and it changed his financial life. He wanted to make an impact in others' lives by helping them the way that Dave Ramsey's program helped him. As he was sharing his plans for his coaching program, I saw myself. In my head, I thought, "Dude, you make no sense!" But it's not easy to tell one of your best friends this.

As we hit some golf balls, I asked, "How much money do you want to make in the first six months?"

He responded, "$7,000."

I then asked, "How much are you charging and how many customers do you need?"

He said, "It would take about forty-seven customers over the next six months to a year."

Something was not adding up. When you start a new business, it is very common to overestimate how many customers you will get. To get forty-seven customers, he might have to talk to two hundred people (if you close 25 percent.) That sounded more like a full-time job. Six to twelve months of work is too much work for $7,000, in my opinion. The hours and time for the return would not be worth it.

In my previous chapter, we discussed hidden costs. Shane told me he was putting in about one hundred hours a month to start the business, roughly five hours a day. This included doing a few hours before work, lunch, and every evening, all while working a full-time job. If we consider six months working one hundred hours per month, it would total six hundred hours. At one hundred dollars per hour for his time, he would amass a cost of $60,000, plus any tech costs, print, and advertising. Let's add another $10,000 for those costs.

Shane said, "As a financial coach, I would never spend $70,000 for $7,000." Ten out of ten people would agree with this statement; however, their strategy must account for your time, not just what you directly pay in currency. Shane was able to adjust his strategy as we spoke. It was impressive.

Often people have a universal response of agreement to any plan someone shares. As a coach, I listen and calculate quickly to see if it makes sense. As I shared my thoughts with Shane, he was receptive. Initially, he was going to charge per hour for his coaching sessions. For someone who is a salaried or hourly employee, this may seem terrific, until you run the numbers like we shared above. Instead, I shared with Shane the value in building his strategy around a high-ticket offer—for him to not trade dollars for hours and to come up with a program. A few weeks later, we connected for another call.

Shane shared with me that his strategy was to develop a $497 online course. In my opinion, I felt it was influenced by Dave Ramsey, which could make it more difficult to sell a premium program. He planned to use click funnels and ads to drive people to his content. I asked Shane, "Who are you targeting?"

He responded, "Anyone who would like to find an extra $1,000 in their budget."

Shane didn't do a deep dive into finding out who his target was. When you clarify your message and value in your strategy, it will allow you to sell for a premium price. I thought Shane had so much value that I encouraged him to distance himself from the Ramsey influence. Dave Ramsey is a financial guru and is wildly successful, but he has scale. He has millions of followers, so when he puts out content for ninety-nine dollars, his audience will buy because of who he is. I asked, "Why would someone pay $497 for a course they can get from Dave Ramsey for $99?" What Shane offered had a personal touch that he could offer a high level of support, which separated him from his competition. His whole outlook was creating complete financial independence. It was starting to make sense.

As we worked through this idea, I shared that he had to do his own deep dive to understand why people should buy from him. There are so many financial coaches that your strategy has to convey unique value. When you explore your value, your limiting beliefs, and the pain that you can solve for clients, it opens the door to commanding high-ticket sales. Your offer becomes a premium offer and your competition only wishes they could charge your rate. They do not understand it. In Shane's strategy, he was not connecting his solution to the impact of financial independence. Part of differentiating your service is helping your prospect connect to the feeling of the new life created by using your product or service.

Shane shared with me his own results from implementing his plan, and it was awe-inspiring. He paid off over $100,000 of debt and now had extra money in the bank. The positive impact flowed through his life and his family. It was amazing. Shane already had a success story in himself, so it was clear his plan worked! I encouraged Shane to have a $5,000 minimum price point.

I asked, "If you were able to hire a coach who could help erase $40,000 of debt for $5,000, using your own funds, would you do it?"

"Of course I would," he replied.

"Would you pay $15,000"?

"Yes!"

In Shane's case, just like in many businesses, initially, his strategy was not built in alignment to hit his goals while connecting the impact of his business. There is nothing more fun than showing someone their service is worth $10,000, not $497. Business owners are blind to this, not because they don't want it, simply because they cannot see it without another perspective.

THE THREE TYPES OF STRATEGIES AND THE ORDER OF OPERATIONS

As a business owner, I love strategy. It's fun for me. It's fun to plan, and it's fun to envision the future. It's fun to think about how you're going to have success as a coach; however, I've watched many organizations continually put together strategies and fail. And the question is, even if they are very well thought out with good numbers and projections, why do strategies fail? We'll look at a couple of different examples to understand what it takes to have a strategy that wins.

The order of operations matters. Strategy is like a math problem but for business. Business strategy refers to the actions or decisions a company takes to reach its business goals and be competitive in its industry. It defines what the business needs to do to achieve its goals, which can help guide the decision-making process for hiring and resource allocation.

I want you to picture a bull's-eye. If you have a bull's-eye or a target, you can aim for it. The strategy says, "This is the bull's-eye, and this is what we aim to hit." If there's no bull's-eye, there's no target. There's no place to gain alignment; there's nothing to aim toward. If you have a target, you have a much higher percentage and chance to hit that target. According to Michael Porter, a Harvard Business professor, economist, and researcher, there are three different types of strategies that a business can have.[26]

---

26   "Michael E. Porter," Harvard Business School, accessed June 5, 2020.

COST LEADERSHIP

The first is cost leadership. Cost leadership is where a firm sets out to become the low-cost producer in its industry.

Many companies get this confused with low prices. Low price follows but only because the cost leader organization controls the production or the supply chain and aggressively negotiates pricing and terms with its suppliers. A great example is Walmart or Costco. Costco controls the cost; it's very aggressive with its suppliers, but that benefits the customer. The same goes for Walmart. Walmart's prices may be a little lower, but it does the same thing. It's a cost leader, and that's a strategy that it's implemented. It drives down costs with its suppliers to pass it on to its customers. Many times, small- and medium-sized businesses try this technique, but they just try to be low cost while not having the power to negotiate and to lower the suppliers' and producers' costs. Eventually, they have no or low profits because they are not charging enough. This is a strategy that often causes businesses to get confused.

DIFFERENTIATING

The second strategy is the differentiating strategy, being different from every other firm. This can be very simple and highly effective. Chick-Fil-A is different because of how it interacts with its people. If you've ever been to a Chick-fil-A, you know they have a signature tagline after any action: "My pleasure."

"It's my pleasure to get you extra napkins."

"It's my pleasure to get you two additional packets of ketchup."

"It's my pleasure to get you a milkshake!"

People remember the friendliness, and they connect with it. "When you're at a Chick-fil-A, you get the feeling that everybody just loves working there."

It does have an excellent product: great chicken! It's great because Chick-Fil-A specializes. You're not going to find a steak there; you're not going to find a burger. Its strategy was to perfect chicken products and the customer experience. It has become very good at it. Chick-fil-A grew sales by nearly $1 billion over the last year, up from the $10.4 billion it made in US sales in 2018.[27]

Differentiating can simply be how you answer the phone. It can be your customer service, your friendliness. It could be how quickly you respond. These are all ways that you can differentiate your business in a crowded, competitive market. The secret is to dive painfully deep into understanding how you are different, creating clarity not only for you but for your customers. When you do this, you will see an increase in sales, because your customers will be clear about what you offer and why they should buy from you.

FOCUS

The third is a focus strategy. The word "focus" can also be synonymous with niche. Ferrari and Lamborghini are high-end car companies and an example of a focus strategy. The

27 Kate Taylor, "Chick-fil-A Is the Third Largest Fast-Food Chain in America, and That Should Terrify Wendy's and Burger King," *Business Insider*, May 14, 2020.

pool of potential customers is a lot smaller, but the company has chosen to put its focus there. Think about the Ferrari or Lamborghini example versus Ford or Chevy or Kia or Honda. The average person can afford a Kia, a Honda, a Ford, or a Chevy. However, they might not be able to afford a Lamborghini or a Ferrari. So, for a car dealership, when it markets, it markets to a much broader audience. You don't see Ferrari or Lamborghini commercials on TV. It doesn't make sense. The return isn't there.

Another example of focus and finding your niche came to me at a carnival. An artist started with a tree stump. He had a chainsaw, and he carved a beautiful eagle sculpture out of this stump. Not many people are going to buy his product. He's in a focused niche, and somebody who wants a custom engraved object or image would hire this guy for a premium because it's a skill. He doesn't have a vast market, but that's his strategy. He's not manufacturing them across the country. For him, his niche is not crowded.

Businesses get in trouble when their market is flooded with the same service and they do not clearly define their expertise. When you're picking a strategy, pick one. Picking one thing to focus on will give you an excellent chance of being profitable. Many firms get stuck and this is why. They don't know their business identity. If you're stuck in the middle and you're taking bits and pieces of different strategies, you're almost guaranteed to have low profitability. So, if you're struggling to be profitable, I bet your strategy is not clear and defined.

Nine out of ten people I talk to believe they are clear with their strategy. They think they're clear with how they differentiate themselves from their competition and their customers. But nine out of the ten are missing the mark. So it's imperative to choose your strategy wisely.

STRATEGY TO CREATE EXPLOSIVE MOMENTUM

"Most people thought I'd only be president for three months. I went from being crazy to visionary." This was what Dr. Stephen Klasko, president of Thomas Jefferson University and CEO of Jefferson Health, said when I was asking him about the organization's explosive momentum.

My relationship with Dr. Klasko started by attending a leadership conference for which he was the keynote speaker. His talk was about how Jefferson was disrupting health care. I thought *He's a guy I would like to meet.* I reached out, and a few weeks later, I was sitting in his office in downtown Philadelphia. The purpose of the meeting was the most fascinating part. I just wanted to introduce myself and hear his story. I was not looking for anything. I did not have a hidden agenda and wasn't trying to sell him on anything.

I'm still not sure why he accepted an in-person meeting, but he did. Maybe for him, it was refreshing to be the CEO of a large organization and have one person who was only needy for knowledge. Connecting with interesting people and hearing their individual stories has been a part of my strategy, and it has led to explosive momentum. When I decided to write a book, I reached out to Dr. Klasko for him to share his insights around my topic of momentum and his strategy that led to explosive growth for Jefferson Health.

When Dr. Klasko became the CEO in 2013, its revenue was $1.6 billion. It had three hospitals, six colleges, 1,200 faculty, 3,100 students, and about fourteen thousand employees.

Five years later in 2018, they were at $5.1 billion in revenue. They had thirteen hospitals, twelve colleges, almost four thousand faculty members, almost eight thousand students, and thirty thousand employees.

This growth doesn't happen by accident.

People want to know the secrets to success and growth. As I spoke with Dr. Klasko, he reflected on a time when he was on the advisory board for iTunes with Steve Jobs. "It hit me, the genius of Steve Jobs. He laid it out so simple. The old math and the new math. The old math represented the operating system and the new math represented a digital lifestyle. At the time, nobody knew really anything about it. That was the 'aha!' moment for me. It was around the year 2000. At the time, I was in Florida, but I began to see and become excited about the opportunity to disrupt the health care system. I realized that many other industries had gone through disruption and the health industry would be next. One of my friends, John Sculley, the former CEO of Apple, talked about Apple's strategy. 'Year one, we change. Year two, we change the industry, and year three, we change the world!' I continued to push the envelope by getting an MBA from The Wharton School of Business. As a doctor, I wanted to remove myself from that way of thinking. I realized we all were learning from the people that screwed up the system. Instead, I studied people like Lee Iacocca, who in the eighties was the CEO of the Chrysler Corporation and was able to transform the auto industry." Frankly, nobody else was doing it.

"When I became CEO of Jefferson, I reflected on all of the work I was already doing. I related what was happening at Jefferson to the old and new math. The old math in health care was academics. The new math was clinical innovation and strategic partnerships. We wanted to create health care with no address.

"We were a very conservative organization when I arrived. I knew I had to make a change. The first thing I did was attend all these town halls. I asked how we get funds. I would ask them, 'If I'm an investor, what gets me excited to invest in Jefferson?' The response was, 'A Premier Academic medical center.' The other response: we were number two to Penn and better than Temple. We were playing in the wrong space and were never going to win that battle, so we took another approach. We took a very external-facing look inside. This journey created our new purpose and strategy. Our mission is we improve lives and our vision is to reimagine health care education and put people first. This strategy has enabled us to create substantial momentum, because it allowed us to focus on areas that other organizations were not, like telehealth.

"In 2013, we invested $35 million into telehealth and people thought we were crazy. We committed to our plan and made 80 percent of our faculty sign up for telehealth. If our departments wanted their incentive, they had to have 80 percent onboard and do one visit per month. They knew they could do it. At the time, seventeen out of eighteen department chairs did it. The one that didn't is no longer a part of Jefferson. Our investment paid off, especially when COVID-19 hit. The organizations that said it wouldn't work are no longer around."

Even after success, there were many times that Jefferson's board was not sure what direction Dr. Klasko was leading them. One of his more rewarding but difficult challenges came when it merged with Philadelphia University. The board could not see or understand why he wanted a fashion, design, and architecture school to join with a medical school. He recalls, "I took every board member out there and had them meet Dr. Spinelli, who was the president at the time. I worked hard to help them see the value. What I saw was the concept of design and innovation merged with health care creating a dynamic force in reimagining health care. It worked."

Jefferson's strategy under Dr. Klasko was clear and drove its record success. It set out to reimagine health care and establish strategic partnerships. It did both and experienced explosive growth. When I asked Dr. Klasko his best advice for organizational strategy, he shared this: "Examine other industries that experienced disruption. Understand how they survived it and where they went wrong. Your industry will experience it. You are either going to lead the change or be forced to change."

He did also note that he believes it is much harder to sustain momentum once you have it. Innovating for someone like Dr. Klasko is the fun part. "Once you stop, you become like everyone else." He highlighted Walmart as an example that continues to innovate to compete with Amazon.

"If you don't double down on innovation and automation, you will become the Sears and Penneys of the world." Dr. Klasko was referring to how Walmart doubled down on innovation and automation to compete in the e-commerce space with Amazon. It had a choice and could have easily stayed in the brick-and-mortar model; however, it might have faded into bankruptcy like many other organizations that did not adapt.

Dr. Klasko and Jefferson Health are a great example of how strategy explodes if you have the first three steps in order. First, Dr, Klasko experienced a deeper dive of awareness when he was on an advisory board with Apple. He continued to build awareness through his time at Wharton. He was able to translate this new way of thinking to value and consider the impact his new way of thinking would have on the health industry. As he continued through the process, he built culture by getting feedback from town meetings and involving board members in ways to help them understand and connect. Finally, to where we are in the book with the seven steps, he implemented a strategy that was primed for success. When he put it in place, it exploded. In the next chapter, we will talk about leadership and, now that you have momentum flowing, how you lead.

INNOVATION STRATEGY

In 2016, I realized that the future was changing rapidly, and it was time to consider adjusting my service business to maximize our success. We did not know that this strategic move set us up to have one of our best years ever, even in a global pandemic!

It all started one day when I walked into our offices, and I saw stacks and stacks of paper everywhere.

These papers were "log sheets" for our service business. They were used to track job time and material used on every job. We also used them to calculate payroll. Everything that a service tech did on a customer's property was documented on these sheets. We were producing so many that we were only reviewing them to process payroll, but we did not review the other data. We were stacks behind on entering the actual versus budgeted amounts. Being behind slowed down our billing. We didn't know if we were winning or losing jobs. We had our overall financials, but that did not show the level of detail per job we needed to be successful.

As an organization, we committed to doing things differently. We realized what we were doing was not sustainable. This was an awareness; we knew that the world was changing and we had to adapt. From there, we did.

In 2016, I established a small test group to experiment with a new platform that was 100 percent digital. Our technicians could get all the job notes, including location, customer requests, log time, and make notes of what they did. They could also see how many hours they had to do the job and, in real-time, see how many hours they had left to finish the job on budget.

We calculated the value this would bring to our organization as well as figuring the overall impact. We realized that not being able to make decisions in real-time had cost some jobs to be 150 percent over budget.

We also recognized the time savings of reducing manual data entry. It allowed our staff to serve customers better and do tasks that continued to move the company forward in reducing manual data entry. Our techs were better informed and needed less instruction from managers because they had all the data at their fingertips. It empowered them with better communication, accountability, and confidence. We talked to our team and our staff and got feedback on the process prior, during, and after our test group. Anytime there's a change, people are going to give resistance or have opinions. I remember the comments. "This isn't going to work. I'm not doing that." In the end, we stayed committed to our plan and we worked to educate our staff on why it was necessary.

We took some of them to an old local gas station that went out of business to help them see what happens when a company does not adjust its strategy. Right beside this gas station was a Sheetz. Sheetz, Inc. is an American chain of convenience stores and coffee shops owned by the Sheetz family. The stores sell a mix of fast food and convenience store items. Nearly all of them sell gasoline. Its headquarters are in Altoona, Pennsylvania.[28]

Sometimes people can't picture what not adjusting your strategy looks like until they can see it. As a kid, I remember stopping at a gas station beside the new Sheetz on our way to my grandparents' cabin. Everyone stopped there. I'm sure from the owners' perspective, they believed that they were invincible. When business was good, they failed to dive deep

---

28 SHEETZ, accessed June 6, 2020.

into understanding how their strategy needed to evolve as years passed. By the time Sheetz moved in, and they called for help, it was too late. We all have an opportunity to stay relevant if we choose. The main trouble is that we all have blind spots that prevent us from truly seeing where we will eventually fail. It's a lot easier to have someone help you before it's too late.

What you will find today is that same lot deserted, boarded up, and looking like a ghost town.

After our pilot test in 2017, we decided to implement a digital system companywide. We kept the paper around as a "backup." We ran with both systems for about seven months until we realized that until the old system was gone, we would never get 100 percent commitment. It was time to let go.

As expected, you will always get some pushback from your staff, but it's essential to educate them on the power, benefits, and reasons why this is good for them.

Going digital was a win for our company because it allowed us to improve efficiency and make adjustments faster by seeing which crews were winning in real-time. The customer won because their delivery improved because the tech had their specific notes at their fingertips. The employee won because, as the company made money, we were able to give bonuses or incentives. All of this elevated the level of service because when you know the target, you can hit it! When you can hit the mark and be successful, it changes your company's morale and spirit.

OUR CORONAVIRUS STRATEGY

Part of our coronavirus strategy was developed in 2016. Fast forward to 2020. The coronavirus was a global pandemic that shook the world.

Nobody was sure what was happening. Nobody was sure how deadly or contagious it was. All we knew was that many businesses had to adjust and adapt. The adjustment was not able to be made by all companies. For many, it was not their choice not to work, but in the end, some went out of business.

Could a different strategy have helped them survive? If they knew or planned for COVID-19, could they have made it through? Many companies don't prepare for a rainy day, and one thing is inevitable: there will be rainy days.

When I reflect and look at 2016, we implemented a strategy, and our approach stayed in place to be relevant to use technology to advance our business.

Sure, we had pain and challenges implementing a new plan, because change is hard. Change takes time and effort, but when the coronavirus hit, we were able to move through pretty seamlessly. It was not easy because many regulations were put in place, but we worked with it.

The CDC limited how many people could work together, how you could function, and what you needed to do.

But at the time, we already had our digital platform setup and were running well. We had a portal for customers, where they could communicate more easily and could order services without having to meet face to face.

The strategy that we put together was so flexible and nimble that it allowed us to work with the challenges. We were able to give our customers the ability to buy without ever having to meet us as a service provider. We allowed techs to take vehicles home, and it all worked because we went digital. No matter where our techs were, they could check in because they had all their workloads right on their mobile device. We streamed right through the pandemic. Not only did we roll through it, but it also turned out to be a benefit because we became even more efficient. After all, we had to leverage the system more. So the coronavirus enhanced the strategy that we put in place in 2016.

Until the pandemic, we were running multiple people on a crew. During the pandemic, we split up teams for safety. It allowed them to be safe, but the data in real-time showed us a significant spike in productivity.

Because of the coronavirus, we were able to see the data improve based on the strategy we had in place.

As technicians saw they were winning and getting rewards, they became more motivated, fueling more company momentum.

So, as you implement or look at your strategy, make sure it's one for the future. If you have an excellent strategy that's flexible and nimble, it will allow you to weather all different storms and adjust as needed. You can be successful during anything and experience rapid growth. Dr. Klasko's early awareness ultimately led him to create a winning strategy that drove explosive momentum, even through the pandemic.

According to Strategy HQ, 90 percent of organizations fail to execute their strategy successfully. Eighty-six percent of executive teams spend less than one hour per month discussing strategy, and 60 percent of organizations don't link strategy to budgeting.[29]

Most strategies don't work because we don't take the time to become aware. Awareness happens when you dive deep into your current market and situation. You must be aware of what's happening in your company as well as what's happening in your industry. Study who failed before but also who succeeded and how they navigated their strategy. Lastly, the most critical part is your self-awareness. Exploring this first will always make sure you do not have any blind spots in your strategy.

If you're a business owner, this will have a direct impact on your organization's success.

This process will create a differentiating strategy because most organizations don't do it this way. You will hear from your people as well as the data, and I promise it will guide you to success!

---

29 Shannon Sage, "Surprising Strategic Planning Stats," OnStrategy, accessed June 17, 2020.

FINAL THOUGHTS

Strategies that work must rely on the individual to research their industry, self, team, and future. When all of this is considered, it puts organizations in place for success. My goal for you is to implement strategies that are longstanding, flexible, and help deliver your mission.

CHAPTER 6

HOW TO STOP
NEGATIVE MOMENTUM

———

"Your present circumstances don't determine where you can go; they merely determine where you start."

—NIDO QUBEIN

Fifteen years ago, it might have ended in a fight.

I maintained my cool because I understand the impact of negative momentum. I try to stop it before it starts, and you can too!

In 2019, my wife and I had extra space in our house and decided to list our space on Airbnb. We were both open to the idea, but she was more reserved than I was. At first, it is a weird feeling to let strangers stay in a part of your house, but we continued.

Airbnb allows homeowners and property owners to list their properties and connect places to stay with travelers. It is a great platform. What we liked best about Airbnb is that hosts can see guests' ratings and reviews. Guests can also see hosts' ratings and reviews. If someone is new to the platform and does not have reviews, the host has the ability to decline the reservation. This helps the host feel comfortable with whom they have staying at their property.

The second benefit to Airbnb is they only charge a 3 percent fee for your listing. We have seen other platforms charge higher percentages and, in the end, it doesn't make it worth it. We have a pretty nice backyard. We have a pool, pavilion, and a putting green that is beautifully landscaped with all-season color and flowers. There is lighting and surround sound. We included this space for the use of guests, which helped drive our value and price.

Our home is located close to Hershey, Pennsylvania. Since so many people travel to Hershey Park, the chocolate factory, and other Hershey attractions, we thought it could be a popular spot. The idea proved correct when we were booked every open weekend in our first year during the summer. The next year, we had our daughter, so that changed a few things. We decided we did not want to do Airbnb anymore with our baby daughter in the house, and at the time COVID-19 was on the rise.

During the 2019 season, we became Airbnb superhosts because of the number of five-star ratings we received. Superhosts are exceptional hosts who are very highly rated. They get rated on cleanliness, value, friendliness, and other areas. It is something we were proud of, that we could share our space with so many people and be a part of their stay in Hershey.

After our daughter and the pandemic, we weren't sure how we were going to travel or vacation. We connected with a guy who just bought an RV and immediately after had health issues and had to sell it. It was basically a brand-new RV because they only had gone on one trip. He was taking a huge loss, and it was a deal we could not pass up. We decided we would use the RV to take family trips. My wife enjoyed the idea of having our own space when we travel. We also decided that instead of letting the RV sit like most people do throughout the year, we would list the RV on Airbnb and capitalize on our superhost status. We made a little campsite with the RV and listed it. The first weekend we listed it, it booked, and the bookings continued to come in.

On our second booking, a couple was staying in the area for the week and the woman decided she wanted to go for a walk. We put the RV and campsite on the back of our property as we have some acreage. Part of our driveway is a shared driveway with the neighbors, and the guests have to drive on that part to get back to the campsite. When the woman walked out of the camper, she made a mistake and walked on our neighbors' property. This prompted a "we have a problem" call from our neighbors.

Up until this point, all of our neighbors got along very well. I reached out to the couple who was staying in our RV to reiterate the boundary to them. They were so nice and apologized and did not want to cause any inconvenience. I assured them that everything was okay. I texted my neighbors to let them know that I had informed our guests. No response. Typically someone responds in some type of way. I thought it was settled until I received the text message: *We need to talk.*

I don't know about you, but I really dislike that phrase. It says nothing except the conversation is probably not going to be fun. The neighbor came over and explained that they had a problem with the driveway that I put in off of the shared driveway. They proceeded to tell me that people should not be on their property. Because of the shared driveway, over the years we both would get each other's mail, packages, and guests. Our only goal was to help whoever or whatever to the correct destination.

When I brought up that we had people too on our property, it was like gas on a fire. My neighbor exploded, and it got ugly quickly. The next couple of days, it seemed to escalate. There were proposed fences, gates, attorneys, surveyors, and everything you could imagine discussed. During each encounter, I maintained my cool somehow. It was hard.

What I knew was negative momentum is much easier to create than positive momentum. This situation with my neighbor could have ignited ten times faster by me choosing to escalate it. Instead, I was able to slow it and stop it by not participating. You don't have to attend every argument you're invited to.

I also was calculating the hidden costs of the matter. Our dispute was over a driveway. All I would have needed to do was say, "I'm not going to use it," and put in a new one. A new driveway would have cost me maybe $5,000. When I added up the cost of battling with my neighbor, it looked like the following

- Legal fees ongoing and court—$10,000
- Adding new driveway to campsite—$5,000
- Changing main driveway—$10,000
- Surveyor, etc.—$1,000
- Ongoing minor disputes—$5,000
- Mental health and stress—$50,000
- Impact on energy level/work impact—$100,000
- Losing friendship of neighbors—priceless

With this quick calculation, I figured this dispute would have an impact of over $180,000. Initially, you may think there is no way, but when you truly track the time, cost, and energy that could linger for five, ten, or twenty years, my number might actually be low. This concept aligns with the hidden costs that most people forget to calculate. Imagine what my life would look like if we continued to battle this situation over the years. When I stop and clearly put a number on the impact of my health, time, and impact it will have on me showing up in my business, it's very easy to see. When you begin to see negative momentum happen, it is important to evaluate the cost of continuing to go down that road. As you explore this, it becomes easier to decide to step away.

My driveway wasn't important, and we considered stopping Airbnb because that is how much we value great neighbors. My neighbor came back and apologized for the actions of the last couple of days and explained that they recently lost a close family member, so it impacted their actions.

In the end, our neighbors are great people, and the hiccup that we had only helped build a deeper level of respect and trust. For any grown adult to come back and apologize with their family is hard, and in my mind, my neighbor is still the winner! It wasn't about pride, because I want to maintain a positive relationship with our neighbors.

Negative momentum happens so quickly. It is important to identify the fuel that is feeding it and remove it. In the situation above, staying cool helped diminish the fire instead of fueling it.

The second step to help stop negative momentum is to put a value on the ongoing cost if you continue forward. Often business owners get stuck on being right and never compare the cost of that choice. It can be extremely expensive.

NEGATIVE MOMENTUM EXISTS!

Most people think about momentum in a positive framework, but momentum can be negative.

Negative momentum is real. I define negative momentum as energy that leads to an undesired result. It exists in business but also in our personal lives.

Once negative momentum starts in the wrong direction, it continues to roll, and it can lead to total devastation if left unattended.

If you watch TV or radio or even listen when you're around friends or family, you probably hear the word momentum more than you think. Pay attention. What is most interesting to me is the fact that we never expand on the topic of momentum. People figure you either have it or you don't.

The problem is that people do not fully understand momentum. They do not know how to implement it or use its power, or they would use it more frequently.

I'm writing this book because I believe there's a tremendous amount of power in momentum—not only in business but connected to your personal life as well. If you can learn how to leverage the power of momentum, it will change your life. The same is true for negative momentum. If you continue to have negative momentum and let it play out, it will change your life but not in a way that most would desire.

The first part is being able to recognize that you are experiencing negative momentum. If you cannot recognize it, you're never going to understand how to reverse this energy. What do I mean by this? It means you have to stop it or slow it down. You have to take negative momentum and turn it into positive.

We all know someone who just can't get it going. It never seems to work out for them, no matter what they do. If one bad thing happens, five more follow. The same pattern occurs in organizations if leadership is not aware or becomes too far removed from its people or customers. In small businesses, those who feel stuck in it may simply have a mindset issue. To say mindset is simple would be misleading. It can be a war within your mind.

David Cuschieri stated, "The mind is a powerful force. It can enslave us or empower us; it can plunge us into the depths of misery, or take us to the heights of ecstasy. Learn to use the power wisely."[30]

What David is talking about relates directly to the mindset for momentum. If your mind is not empowering you, it's enslaving you. If you're not aware of its powers, by default it may enslave you, so understanding it is essential. Think about one of your friends or family members who has negative momentum. It is probably pretty easy for you and many others to see the mistakes they're making. You may even wonder why they don't just stop. However, they are enslaved by their mind and, as silly as it may seem, might not be able to see the problem.

In the awareness and mindset chapter, we dive into the importance of awareness and how it is connected to mindset. Awareness is the foundation of starting momentum in both your personal and business life. You can refer back to that chapter at any time, as it will be the foundation of your success.

Going back to the friend example, if that same friend uses their mind to empower themselves, they can get the desired outcome. They may not get the result initially, but they will over time. The longer you're on this negative ride, the harder it is to stop. But before you can have positive momentum, you must bring any negative momentum to a minimum or stop.

I want you to envision two train tracks—one that goes east and one that goes west. There are two trains lined up parallel.

---

30 Goodreads, David Cuschieri, accessed June 19,2020.

Train number one goes east for one hundred yards and gains a speed of ten miles per hour, and then it puts on the brakes.

Train number two goes west for five miles and gains a speed of one hundred miles per hour and then puts on the brakes.

These examples can both represent people who have negative energy. Train number one recognizes it and puts on the brakes. It barely got any speed, and it's able to stop very quickly. In my prior example with my neighbor, it was only a couple of days and then the brakes were put on. The negative energy was stopped.

Train number two gets going and doesn't recognize or doesn't address the negative momentum. They could be choosing to feed it. By the time it puts on the brakes, it's five miles down the road and going one hundred miles per hour. This train will take over one mile to stop entirely. Not only does it take more time, but it can also cause more damage along the way. The longer that downward spiral goes, whether it's a mental health issue or a bad habit that needs to stop, there is likely damage occurring along the way, which multiplies exponentially the longer the negative momentum exists.

The faster you can identify negative momentum, the quicker you can get to a stop and then create positive energy.

Negative momentum can show up in many ways. It can be personal stress, it can be reduced cash flow in your business, or it can be a negative work culture. Below is a chart of symptoms of negative momentum.

SYMPTOMS OF NEGATIVE MOMENTUM

Loss of morale

Loss of motivation

Attrition

Lack of retention

Slow growth

Not attracting top talent

Higher costs

Unproductivity

Selfishness

Negativity

Being short on cash

Imposter Syndrome

Bringing work home

Affecting spouse

Irritability w/kids

More work, less pay

Poor work culture

Loss of hope

Anger

Always being on call

Being behind on bills

Worsened reputation

Slow sales

Feeling unworthy

Shame

Helplessness

Upset vendors

Fear of losing business

Anxiety

Self-worth diminishing

Loss of opportunity

Clients knowing

Loss of faith

Loss of purpose

No profit

Limiting beliefs

Confusion

Market slipping away

Boredom

Health effects

Feeling mentally drained

Loss of control

No way out

Lack motivation

Seeing less progress the harder you work

No one to talk to

Poor client retention

Blind spots

Any of the above lead to a constant up-and-down in business—wondering why you do what you do.

These are all examples of negative momentum. If any of these resonate with you, you have to do a deep dive to see why this is showing up and what's causing it. Why are you allowing it to continue? When are you going to choose to stop?

We have to get the negative momentum to stop before moving on to start the positive momentum.

HOW DO WE STOP NEGATIVE MOMENTUM?

Negative momentum stops when you evaluate your mindset. It is stopped by looking at the root belief about why you feel or think a certain way about a situation. In my neighbor example, I was able to keep my cool when I truly understood the value of the situation. Changing the lens of how you view a situation is a great way to slow or stop negative momentum. Knowing that my neighbor recently lost a close family member could have also influenced my lens, as he was out of character. Anything that helps put a neutral viewpoint on a situation can help keep you balanced during times of dispute.

The same is true for individuals. If you know you have a problem but do not take action to fix it, you will continue to stay on the crazy cycle of up and down. This is true in business or in your personal life.

I CHOOSE MY LENS

My father wanted nothing to do with me. He chose a life without me in it. It's sad but true.

I remember making the call. I was nineteen years old. Up until that point, I had never met my father. My life was pretty good for the most part. I had a loving mother and grandma and grandpa who supported me as a kid. The absence of a father wasn't something that I really thought about. My mom made it clear throughout the years that I could get in contact with him at any time. She would say, "Seth, if you want to meet your father, I'll help you." I declined. For whatever reason, it wasn't important to me. I think inside I felt like it would add extras to my life, and I enjoy a relatively simple life. What if he was a really nice guy? There would be extra people to see. What if it turned out bad? What if he didn't want to see me? Maybe it had to do with the fact that I lived with a verbally abusive stepdad and that was all I knew. I couldn't take two of them. There was always that chance.

As I grew up, I was involved in sports and my local church. Through all different stages of my life, I had outstanding male role models who took me under their wing, from elementary, middle school, high school, and even college. The combination of good men filled that void and all of them contributed to my momentum. I believe I was fortunate. I got to see the best qualities of these men in my life as mentors and role models. I watched how they treated their families and the high standards they set for themselves. This had a huge impact on me—possibly more so than if I'd had a true father in my life.

But there still came a point that it was time to reach out to my real father. A father is still a father and it was time. I was at a point in my life where I already had my service business, and my life was pretty good. I had been on my own for about three years, and I thought the dust had settled pretty nicely.

I remember being at peace with whatever happened. I remember thinking, *I'm ready for this.* I didn't tell anyone that I was going to reach out. I looked up my father's name in the yellow pages (yes, the yellow pages) and I remember seeing the letters extra clearly. Yes, that was him. I paused. I picked up the phone and pressed the numbers. I felt each number on my fingertips as I pressed it. When the phone didn't ring right away, I thought maybe I missed a number. I'm not sure I would have dialed again if it didn't ring, but it rang.

The rings felt slow and like hours apart. Just as I thought I'd hang up, a woman answered the phone. Why didn't I think of this? The whole time I practiced with my father answering the phone. It completely threw me off. My mind raced. *Does she even know about me? I can't say who I am?* I decided not to hang up and said, "Is Everett there?"

I finally did it! It felt good. I felt relief in that moment until her response.

She said, "I'm sorry. He passed away."

I swallowed hard and timidly said, "I'm sorry... bye." My heart sank.

Now my casual approach turned into a mission. I informed my mom, and she helped me pull documents, the obituary, and map out relatives and connections. It now felt like an FBI case.

I located Cory, my brother, whom I never knew I had, and made the phone call. I felt like I was on a late-day talk show when I said, "Hi, I'm your brother that you didn't know you had. I have all the paperwork and the birth certificate with our dad listed on it. I don't want anything. A few weeks ago, I tried to reach out to our dad and found out he died before I could meet him."

There was a long silence but after we talked Cory said, "I need to call my sister, Lisa. I'm sure she's going to want to talk or maybe even meet."

And sure enough, he was right. Lisa sent me tickets to visit.

As I arrived at Penn Station, I was walking up the steps not knowing whom I was looking for. It was one of the most interesting feelings to be looking for the people I didn't know, who were family, and whom I would be staying with for the whole weekend. Read that again.

The weekend turned out great, and through that call and weekend, I met Lisa, Cory, and his two daughters, Angelica and Arielle. They are amazing people, and I'm so glad I made that call and decided to pursue learning about my family.

I share this because even though I had a challenging childhood at times with a verbally abusive stepdad, I chose to always view life and people as good. I experienced negative momentum in many areas of my life, but I chose to never let it get me completely down. I always recognized negative momentum and worked to stop it or get away from it as soon as possible. A perfect example is me moving out of my house at sixteen years old to remove myself from the environment my stepdad created.

I've been fortunate; I'm thankful for everyone who contributed along my journey. We all have a choice and the mindset that we choose will either fuel negative momentum or stop it and begin a journey of abundance and positivity.

BAD START TURNED CHAMPION

One of my best friends, Shane Woodman, shared a story that aligned with this. I met Shane in a class at Penn State Harrisburg in 2007. Shane was on the golf team at Penn State Harrisburg and was the number two player. I do not know all the rules of golf, but he explained that typically the best four or five players would play a competitive match and represent the school. One tournament stood out, as he recounted to me.

The night before the NEAC (North Eastern Athletic Conference) tournament, he was in his apartment in Middletown, Pennsylvania. By now, it was May 2011. He was nervous, but he was ready. He realized the next day could be the last time he ever played collegiate golf. The pressure was building. That night, he slept as well as anyone could expect to sleep when the next day there was such a monumental event.

As he drove to the course, he reflected on what his coach Brad Kane had told him over his four years of being a golfer.

He would often say, "Try and beat the people in your group. That's the only thing you can control and try to set the pace with everybody that you're competing against that is next to you." This advice helped in the past.

Shane set a goal of shooting seventy-seven. Par on a golf course is typically seventy-two, which means that throughout the course, you have seventy-two hits over eighteen holes to meet the regulation. Anything over seventy-two is over par.

The day was perfect for golf; it was sunny, clear skies, and about seventy-five degrees. It could not have been better. There were eight schools involved in the tournament with four or five players from each. Shane started at hole number nine.

He teed the ball at the first tee box and ripped the drive down the fairway, and the nerves went away. He finished his first hole with a bogey. That means that if the goal was to get the ball in the cup in four strokes, he did it in five. The lousy start played with his mental state. He went on to play some of the worst golf for the next eight holes. He played with no confidence and was experiencing negative momentum. Small mistakes and bad shots were compounding, and he didn't want it to end this way. He reminded himself that this could be the last time he would ever wear a Penn State Harrisburg golf uniform.

At this point, Shane was five over par and was entering hole number one. He parred number one. Then he struck a perfect eight iron four feet from the next cup—birdie for hole number two!

He could feel it. The negative momentum was stopping, and he was starting to build positive momentum and energy.

Now it was time to keep it going. By hole number six, Shane was in a groove. He passed one of his golf teammates, Jeff, and they gave each other the thumbs up.

Jeff was always the number one player, and Shane was usually the number two player.

As Penn State Harrisburg went on to win the North Eastern Athletic Conference Championship, Shane became emotional and tears streamed from his face. Three and a half years of coming in second place had taken a toll on his mental state. Emotional, he called his dad and said, "We are NEAC champs! We're going to North Carolina!"

His dad proudly paused and said congratulations. Then he asked, "How did you play? "

In Shane's story, it took three and a half years to finally tilt the seesaw to the other side. Once he broke through this barrier, his winning mindset carried over into the business world.

Currently, Shane is the sales manager for Onspot US and Canada, where he manages five team members. He has been with the company since 2016. He started as a sales manager and was promoted to sales manager of the entire sales force in 2018.

Shane understood negative momentum differently after his experience on the golf course in that unforgettable tournament. He understood how to overcome it. He understood that negative momentum attacks when the stakes are the highest. Typically, it is never about skills. I've watched some of the most skilled people fail because of their mindset. Mindset enables you to burst through when negative momentum attacks.

Shane believes to get momentum you have to start with small pieces. "Set small objectives along the way to your goal. As you achieve each small objective, it provides you a little more momentum toward the end goal. It is crucial to plan with the end in sight." Shane recommends reading and applying *The 7 Habits of Highly Effective People* by Stephen Covey. In addition to this book, Shane also recommends starting with the end in mind. For him, the end was the seventy-seven in the golf story. He ended up shooting a seventy-five, two better than his goal.

Shane put small wins together on that golf day and continued to do it in his professional career. In 2019, his company implemented a momentum tracker. They realized they were missing key opportunities in the sales funnel process but didn't have a system in place to track these. Once the momentum tracker was set up, it was easy for everyone on the team to see where each member was at a glance and to know where to focus their efforts. This started momentum for Shane's company.

As the snowball of momentum gains traction, it gets bigger and bigger as it goes down the hill. The more goals you accomplish, the bigger the ball is rolling down the mountain. All of this happens because of creating small, measurable wins, just like that day on the golf course. Make sure to recognize when negative momentum creeps in and work to shift the mindset to start positive momentum.

Shane's story is an example of how he was able to recognize that he was off to the wrong start, and in a short time turned what seemed to be a loss into a win through positive momentum.

CHAPTER 7

LEADERSHIP

"I realized I was more convincing to myself and to the people who were listening when I actually said what I thought, versus what I thought people wanted to hear me say."

—URSULA BURNS

STRONG LEADERSHIP MAKES GUIDING YOUR ORGANIZATION EASY.

"Everyone knows I'm the boss. That's the way it has to be, to be successful." When Herb said this to me, he wasn't being prideful. His message was clear that successful organizations have clear leadership and someone who is without a doubt in charge.

Herb Magee was my basketball coach when I played for Philadelphia University. Herb became the coach of Philadelphia Textile in 1967 after being a player, assistant coach, and then a short run at the NBA. If you are not sure who Herb Magee is, he is a legend in the basketball community. In fifty-three seasons, he has won 1,123 games, which makes him one of the winningest basketball coaches in college basketball history. For perspective, Mike Krzyzewski, the famous Duke men's basketball coach, had 1,132 at the time of this book. Herb Magee is in the Naismith Basketball Hall of Fame with the likes of Michael Jordan, Larry Bird, and Wilt Chamberlain.

Herb has had hundreds of players, assistants, and new administrators during his tenure as the head man for the Philadelphia University—now the Jefferson—men's basketball team, but the only thing that hasn't changed is his leadership and consistent winning. In all those years, Herb's teams have averaged twenty-one wins per season out of twenty-eight games. When I initially spoke with Herb about momentum, he said, " I'm not sure you can control momentum."

I didn't agree with him, but I wanted to see how the conversation would evolve. My first question was, "How? How did you do it? It is remarkable to basically never lose." Countless coaches start coaching and start winning because of their initial hype but soon fade off and get fired as they lose momentum. Not Coach Magee.

The first thing Herb said was, "It's the ingredients of your team. All of my best teams had special character. I'm not talking about the starting lineup, I'm talking about all twelve guys, one through twelve."

I can attest to the relationships I formed from the team. My best man at my wedding, Malcolm Ingram, was someone I met my freshman year. Everything Herb described aligned with the high character of Malcolm and many of the other players. "They have the right attitude; they are there for their teammates, and they do what the coach tells them"

One team that stood out for Herb was his National Championship team. It was his third year as a head coach, and the team started by losing to Villanova and then in double overtime to Mount Saint Mary's. Then it went on to win twenty-eight straight games and the Division 2 National title. During this run, the team beat its opponents by an average of twenty-three points. When I asked Herb what made them different, he went back to a special character. I asked him to elaborate more.

He said, "Each guy on that team knew their role and they did it. They came to practice 100 percent every day and had tremendous respect for their teammates." Another team Herb mentioned was the team of Patrick Chambers and Ed Mallory. Patrick Chambers was the head men's basketball coach at Penn State University, and Ed Mallory is one of the top NBA officials. "That team was great as well; they lost in the tournament, but they had a shot.

"Many teams have talent, in fact, most do, but not all have the proper character." He went on to say, "I watch how prospects react to referees, treat their coaches, talk to their parents. This tells me who they really are, and I've been pretty right about it over the years."

Once Herb built a team, the next most important part was for everyone, whether it be coaches, players, or managers, to know Coach Magee was in charge. Everyone knows that things will go according to what Coach says. He clarified that it's not about "forcing it into their head every day but it's an understanding. If you have great senior leadership, it transfers as the new freshmen come in. The cycle repeats itself if a leader does their job. It really makes it easier and enjoyable. My best teams had great leaders."

He pointed out a few professional organizations that continue to struggle and compared them to ones that won. First, he highlighted the New York Knicks. "They just changed coaches again… They've hired great coaches but still cannot win, so you have to look at leadership. Ultimately ownership is in charge."

He compared the New York Knicks to the Boston Celtics and the impact Danny Ainge had since becoming the general manager. He noted Danny Ainge brought in Brad Stevens as a great coach and made moves that benefitted the organization as a whole. The Boston Celtics organization is winning again, but it started with awareness of the leadership to know they needed a change. Herb also mentioned the New England Patriots football team. "Everyone knows who is in charge of their organization; it's Bill Belichick." For organizations that do not have momentum, Herb said, "I would really question if the person that says they are in charge is really in charge or demonstrates true leadership. Leaders set the tone of the organization. Managers manage against what is outlined by leadership."

I can attest to this being true. Not only was Herb Magee a clear leader, but when I played for Herb Magee in 2007, we had an amazing team. What stands out the most to me is the character of the players. In all the teams that I have ever been on, we had a very special team captain—so much so that even to this day, I still tell his story. Moe Martin was the best team captain I have ever played for on any team. Character is shown the most in times of challenge, and this was definitely the situation for Moe.

The season prior, Moe was a starter on the basketball team, and he played the entire game every game that year. The year I arrived, Moe was promoted to captain, but that same year, Christian Burns arrived. Christian transferred from Division 1 Quinnipiac University and eventually went on to become the national Division 2 player of the year that year. With the excitement of becoming the team captain, Moe Martin also got the gut-wrenching news that Christian was going to take his spot in the starting lineup. Coach is well known for only playing five players during the game, so if you were not in the starting lineup, you might not have gotten to play in the game.

From that moment, I watched Moe Martin show up every day to be positive and lead our team. I'm sure it was against all the voices in his head, but he was energetic, encouraging, and did what was best for the team. As I watched him barely play all season, his character showed bright and still stays with me today as a great example of sacrificing yourself for what is best for the team and doing so with a positive attitude.

That year, we lost in the NCAA tournament, but as I spoke with Herb Magee about his success, I realized that the secret to his momentum was his process of recruiting character and demonstrating clear leadership.

By the end of our conversation, Herb said, "I guess there is a formula for momentum. I never really thought about it this way."

My goal for everyone reading this book is to examine the steps to control your own momentum. Winning over 1,123 games, coaching for fifty-three years, and winning over twenty-one games per season is clearly momentum. Sometimes you just have to look at the steps and then repeat!

LEADERSHIP MAY NOT KNOW HOW TO WIN

Ernie Accorsi was in the front row at Eli Manning's retirement announcement at the New York Giants facility. As Eli held two Super Bowl trophies, it was evidence Ernie knew how to build a winning organization.

"Not everyone knows how to win," said Ernie. "Organizations get lulled into mediocrity. They think if they have a winning record over ten years but no championship that is success. You create an attitude of being used to losing." Ernie Accorsi has a storied NFL career. He was a general manager for the Colts, Browns, and New York Giants. He hired Bill Belichick, the eventual Hall of Fame football coach, when he was the general manager for the Browns. He was around greats like Vince Lombardi, whom the Super Bowl Trophy is named after. He's in the Pennsylvania Sports Hall of Fame with Wilt Chamberlain, Arnold Palmer, and Joe Montana. He was inducted into the New York Giants Ring of Honor, which is his most prized personal accomplishment.

It's clear Ernie knows how to win, so I asked him what he witnessed over his successful career. "Winners know how to win. When I was a public relations assistant under Joe Paterno and Penn State football shortly after college, we were playing Kansas State in 1969. That week, Joe said that they were going to be the fastest team we ever saw on AstroTurf. They had just beaten Oklahoma forty-four to twenty. We were coming into the game with a twenty-eight-game win streak from the last two seasons. As a rookie, I asked George Welsh, the offensive coach at the time, 'Can we beat them?' He looked at me and said. 'They aren't going to beat us; they can't beat us. You watch. We'll make a big play and it will break their backs. They don't truly believe they can beat us.' A few hours later, I was in the press box during the game and said, 'Do we have a chance?' His response was, 'Joe will find a way to win it.' We ended up winning the game fifteen to fourteen."

Great leadership instills a confidence in your team that gives you a competitive advantage. Leadership is the fifth step to building momentum for a reason. Without the first four steps, you will not build sustainable momentum. Leadership begins with mindset and awareness. All steps are a must to build ongoing explosive success. In chapter one, we pointed out how approximately 80 percent of your life is on autopilot and controlled by your subconscious mind. Even if 20 percent of your verbal intent is saying you believe you can win, it will always be stalled by the 80 percent subconscious telling you that you will lose. We have witnessed this with teams or organizations that always seem to fumble or lose in the end. Some organizations will come back and win in almost any situation. They understand the value of their decision, have the right culture, and stick to their strategy.

"I took a lot of criticism for my decision to draft Eli Manning because Kerry Collins had taken us to the Super Bowl. He was a great quarterback and very popular with our fan base, but as a leader, I owned it. I felt we had to upgrade the QB position to another level. Another piece of the puzzle was adding Tom Coughlin. Rumors and writers were saying we would never get free agents because no one wants to play for Coughlin, even though he had a winning track record coming from Jacksonville. But once he came on as coach, I never had a free agent that I really wanted that we didn't get.

"The players that are worth bringing in want discipline. When I signed Plaxico Buress from the Steelers, he lifted our whole organization. He had the Super Bowl-winning catch in the 2015 season. The decisions I made were always to take us from good to great. I'm not a stats guy, and I don't care about quarterback ratings. I don't care about any of that stuff. There's only one reason you hire a head coach. There's only one reason you draft a quarterback. That's to win a championship. That's all. If you had a terrific career and threw for a million yards but didn't win a championship, if I drafted you high in the first round, my draft choice fell short."

These are tough comments, but driving excellence in organizations takes this type of focus. Once you establish your standard, it becomes easier. It builds confidence and the expectation of winning, like Ernie experienced at Penn State. Ernie also shared a few Vince Lombardi stories. Vince Lombardi was the famous head coach of the Green Bay Packers and won five Super Bowls in nine seasons. After Vince Lombardi's success in Green Bay, he became the Washington Redskins' head coach. Just the announcement of him becoming the new coach caused Sonny Jurgensen, the Redskins quarterback, to decide to lose twenty-five pounds before training camp. That is the impact a proven winner has on an organization.

As I continued to listen to Ernie talk, his insight was amazing, but the question that I wanted to know was, "What happens if you do not have this structure and a proven track record?" Everyone knows that if Bill Belichick walks in to coach a team or Oprah walks onto a set, what they say is the final word. They have established their credibility and it is easier to lead from that place. Obviously, they all worked to get to that point, but how?

Ernie reflected back to Vince Lombardi when he first became the head coach of the Green Bay Packers. Prior to this, he was only an assistant, so he had no real credibility. Vince Lombardi set the standard and demanded it. "There's a lot of famous stories of Vince Lombardi walking in and saying, 'We're going to win here, these are the rules and the party's over. If you don't like it, you can get out.' Well, people started leaving. The players started to leave because they didn't want to be a part of it. The ones who left are the ones you do not want in your organization. The ones that stay are who you need. One player, Bart Starr, said in one of his books that he called his wife that night and said 'We're gonna win.'"

Too many times we are afraid to hold people accountable, and staying average continues to show up in an organization's sales, client retention, employee retention, and ultimately the bank account.

Your goal as an organization should be to win a championship, whatever that is for your organization. First, you have to define it. Understand your blind spot to the success you want. From there, it's understanding the new value in your mission. When you get your team behind you, it leads to explosive momentum, but you must commit to your strategy. This means if you have a few losing seasons in order to win it all, that is okay. Teams that always have a winning record but no championship are weak in leadership. If you are new to leadership, you must realize that you must find great talent. Invest in talented employees but hold them accountable. You must demand or your team will call your bluff. This was one of my blind spots and weaknesses. What I allowed I received. When I demanded excellence, people left, service improved, and talent wanted to be a part of our new mission. In addition, if you are an owner, you must give your general manager power. If you are a board, you must give your CEO power. If the team can access the board without the CEO, you will undermine your success and experience stalled momentum. Your organization must know who is in charge. In the Giants' example, ownership hired a general manager, Ernie, whom it believed in. It gave him the authority to make the moves for the organization. Ernie hired a coach he believed in and gave the authority to run the team his way by demanding results and holding people accountable. The team attracted the best talent, and it has championships to show for it. These types of organizations have a history of winning because of their mindset and approach to leadership. It's time for you to win a championship. You just have to demand it.

LEADERSHIP FROM A WORLD VIEW

Princess Diana was world-famous: the Princess of Wales. In 1987, she visited an AIDS patient in a hospital in London. There was a famous picture of the moment, which went viral because the picture shows Princess Diana shaking the hand of the AIDS patient. It was a monumental day in the news when this took place. Today, this may not seem like much, but in 1987, AIDS was a disease that was not understood. Many people thought that if you were around a person with AIDS, you could get it.

Princess Diana had a choice. She had limited information just like many of us in business before the facts are common knowledge. She decided at that moment with the information she knew to make a statement about breaking this barrier. What Princess Diana did was break down that barrier by taking a chance in having contact with this patient. It was a choice between the unknown and the known. As a leader, she set an example and changed the world forever with this simple gesture. As a leader, the simplest gestures, reactions, and responses can send massive impacts throughout your organization or with your customers. People are watching how you lead and what you do

When I think of a leader, I think of somebody who simplifies the process. They can predict or envision the future. They provide structure. Leaders provide systems—they delegate, or they elevate others.

It was almost like Princess Diana had a crystal ball and could see into the future that it was time for a change surrounding the fear to embrace acceptance of people with AIDS.

Though it was controversial at the time, she was far ahead of her time, and many people did not understand. When leaders make decisions in alignment with areas they are passionate about, results happen, including making the world a better place.

Being a leader is sometimes a lonely job; it's highly questioned and criticized. In today's world, leaders are in the spotlight and face the most scrutiny for how they handle situations and their responses. Social media can change a person's whole career. There's so much pressure on leaders, so it's essential to understand what leaders should be doing.

PROMOTION DOES NOT EQUAL LEADER

A few months ago, I was talking to an engineer.

I asked how his job was going. This is the typical "start a conversation talk" when you meet somebody.

I always spend a little extra time trying to understand what's going well and what may be a challenge for them. Any insight that I can gain has proved highly valuable in my career.

There is power in asking questions. I frequently ask questions of my staff, my mentors, and other leaders. Questions unlock so much information in unexpected ways. I find that people are so knowledgeable, and anytime I can tap into that, I do.

The engineer began to share his insights.

He proceeded to tell me how he does not enjoy managing a group of other engineers. I asked, "How did you get to that position?" It would seem like that would have been the ideal role that he worked toward achieving.

He said, "Well, I started as an engineer, and I was doing an excellent job in my role. So they promoted me. They made me look over a couple of other engineers."

I fired off a couple of questions: "How'd that make you feel, what did you enjoy? Did they give you support?"

He responded, "No, they kind of just threw me into the fire, and I just had to do it without much training."

I continue to see examples of promotion by success, which I call the promotion of death. An employee does an excellent job in their role, and then you get promoted to be a manager or supervisor. The problem is that you, most likely, never had training, but now all of a sudden, you're a leader. You became a leader, by promotion, and you didn't do anything to improve the skills you would need for the next role. Leadership is something that takes a lot of time and energy to develop.

Leaders are not born; they are made through experiences, practice, and ongoing learning. Some might have more skills than others, but it isn't something that you're just naturally good at, all around.

I remember interviewing an individual who was applying to be a manager for one of my companies. As I was doing the interview, I asked, "How did you become a manager at your other job?" They proceeded to tell me it was because they did a good job. I then asked if they received any leadership training, and they said no. This told me I would really have to examine if they had what it took to be a manager because they had no training.

What is the difference between a manager and a leader? A manager is a mechanic and mechanics are very, very important. I'm not downplaying their importance because what they do is extremely important. Management and leadership are just two separate skills.

In baseball, you need a pitcher, and you need a catcher for the game to work. In basketball, you need a point guard to handle the ball and the center to block shots and rebound the ball. They are equally important.

The same is true in business. Both are important and essential for business success, but a manager is somebody who's more task-focused. They are someone who has subordinates. Managers look to get things done; they administer a process. They look to meet objectives and delegate tasks.

A good manager is skilled at allocating work.

Managers like to maintain the status quo. A good manager isn't looking for much change. They're looking to deliver the job that they are assigned to do. If they were assigned to manage a business unit or department, their goal is to manage it successfully. They do not want to shake things up; they just want to maintain the mission.

Leaders, on the other hand, look to innovate. They're people-focused.

They have followers who naturally want to follow them. People around them gravitate to them. Leaders focus on doing the right thing; they have a higher purpose; they can "see" into the future. When I say see into the future, it doesn't mean they have a crystal ball, but they're looking to see what's on the horizon that they need to adjust for. What is the organization leading toward? What is the change that's coming?

The above is what leaders do. When we look back at Princess Diana's example, even though it is not a business example, it's an excellent example of a form of leadership.

LEADERSHIP CAN MISS THE MARK

Raise your hand if you have ever gone to a conference in a large office building. You know the type. One that has multiple levels with mostly office space and a few larger conference rooms. If you are lucky, the building will have a few nice amenities like clean bathrooms, comfortable furniture, and maybe a cafe or lounge. Pretty standard, right?

So you would think. I attended a Future of Work conference in Charlotte, North Carolina, in October 2019. I became interested in the Future of Work after speaking with Jason Reilly and having some conversations with Deloitte. I realized I had already been doing some of this work in my organizations, although I did not know its official label. I believe it is important to look to the way the future workplace will change and stay ahead of it. This will create a competitive advantage for your organization. I thought I would be walking into the "typical" conference setting that we've all been to. However, what I walked into blew my mind when I found outdoor basketball courts, a bowling alley, cafe, and, my personal favorite: a self-serve coffee machine complete with a touch screen and freshly ground beans. It could make you any type of coffee you liked. I was so amazed; I immediately texted a picture to my wife and it went straight onto her Christmas list.

Throughout the conference, I spent every spare minute exploring the building. I thought it must be like paradise to work there with all of the extra perks. But when I finally got the opportunity to ask the employees for myself over lunch, they said, "It's not as great as it looks."

Their coworkers proceeded to tell me the company had missed the mark and spent massive amounts of money in areas that the employees frankly didn't want. It actually created resentment because they were not able to use it thanks to the demanding work schedule. However, their bosses were able to find time for a game of basketball during the day.

How could the company not be in touch with their people? How? Why didn't someone simply ask them what was important to them? The company seemed to be willing to spend for employee benefit, but the money appeared to be vain.

I followed up and asked. "What would help you?" I was expecting an unreasonable question like a hot tub in each office or something ridiculous. I was surprised to find much more minor requests like having a company shuttle from the closest bus stop that was about half a mile away.

Looking from the outside, I would assume this company was crushing it—it had momentum, but when I got inside, I realized it didn't. From that moment, I set out on a journey and looked to explain the question. How do companies actually build an organization that creates true momentum?

MINI EXAMPLE

I was at one of our facilities, and in our service and construction business, we have heavy equipment.

A couple of days in a row, I was at the facility, and an individual asked a supervisor to move a heavy piece of equipment.

The supervisor continued to move this same piece of equipment day after day. In a manager's mind, they're helping fix the problem that is right in front of them. They view the situation as keeping the technician going by removing the barrier for that day.

After watching this play out a couple of days, it repeated itself once more. Only this time, the supervisor was not there, and I was the closest person in sight. "Can you move this heavy piece of equipment?" he said.

My automatic response was, "Get in the seat! It's time for you to learn how to move this piece of equipment." Leaders think differently, and they look to solve problems not only for today but forever.

This individual will be able to move the piece of equipment that was in his way for the rest of his life. Knowledge is power, and leaders empower others to be great.

When I work with business owners, I find they're spending 75 to 90 percent of their time managing instead of leading. When we can switch that ratio, it helps change the outcome of their business and organization.

VISIONARY LEADERSHIP

Elon Musk is an excellent example of a leader, and it may be an extreme example, but it helps show and demonstrate what a leader should be doing. Elon Musk was a co-founder of PayPal; eBay eventually purchased PayPal in 2002 from Musk, propelling him to billionaire status.[31]

Musk is an entrepreneur but also a visionary. He started SpaceX. SpaceX is a private spaceflight company that puts satellites into orbit and delivers cargo to the International Space Station (ISS). It was the first private company to send a cargo satellite to the ISS, doing so in 2012. The company is working on developing powerful rockets and spacecraft capable of carrying people into space.[32]

In an interview in 2012 on *60 Minutes*, Elon Musk shared his insights into why he started SpaceX.

Musk believed that space exploration should be a low-cost option and that it is essential for mankind to be able to connect to outer space.[33]

As you're reading these words, they may sound confusing, or even weird, but growing up, Elon Musk's hero was John Glenn and a few other astronauts.

---

31   Margaret Kane, "eBay Picks up PayPal for $1.5 Billion." *CNET*, August 18, 2002.

32   Elizabeth Howell, "SpaceX: Facts about Elon Musk's Private Spaceflight Company," Space.com (Future US Inc,), December 16, 2019.

33   "2012: SpaceX: Elon Musk's Race to Space." *60 Minutes Rewind*, December 9, 2018, video, 14:35.

He set out on this mission to make it affordable to go to space. Before this, no privately funded shuttle took off, went into space, and returned safely.

He set out to do this as a broader mission for humanity and to make his heroes proud. During the process, many longtime astronauts, businesses, and other organizations criticized Musk, because they viewed him as an outsider. Here's a guy that one day just decided to go to space because he was a "kid" (forty years old) with money while others dedicated their whole life to space.

They said that he wouldn't be able to do it.

They said it was a waste of time. They said he wouldn't do it safely.

On March 29, 2020, his shuttle took off with two astronauts headed to the International Space Station. The journey was long, the journey was hard, and as a leader, he received criticism from those he wanted approval from most.

He fought through it all and believed in his vision—the vision that nobody else could see the way he could. He did it.

Leadership is hard. Leadership is tough.

Even though Musk is a leader, he still had many managers on his team to help keep the day to day going. But the same principle of looking out for others, caring about people, and seeing into the future that other people cannot see, just like how Princess Diana is a vital part of leadership that people miss.

MAMBA MENTALITY/OVERNIGHT SUCCESS

Kobe Bryant is regarded as a tireless competitor but also as a leader. Kobe Bryant was a player in the NBA for a decorated twenty-year career from 1996 to 2016 for the Los Angeles Lakers. He came up with the mantra Mamba Mentality. Unfortunately, Kobe passed away in a tragic helicopter accident in 2020 with his daughter and a crew of other people. The whole world paused to honor his accomplishments.

People lead in different ways. Some people are vocal, some lead by action. He was a leader through his actions. His mantra of Mamba Mentality is about 4 a.m. workouts, doing more than the next guy, and trusting in the work you put in when it's time to perform.

Without studying, preparation, or practicing, you're leaving the outcome to fate.

But I would argue that all leaders have a sense of Mamba Mentality, even though entrepreneurs may not be athletes. The mantra still applies. There are countless stories of Elon Musk sleeping in his building because he worked tirelessly at his craft. Leaders and other people across the globe can relate to putting in the time when nobody is watching.

We've all heard of the overnight success. It doesn't exist! If you talk to anybody successful, the journey to success is tough and usually a long road. As you rise to the top, just like the engineer story, now you are expected to lead. Leadership takes lots of time, practice, energy, support from mentors, and coaching.

It's a lot of work.

When I was a freshman at Philadelphia University, I already owned a company for four years with four to six employees.

During the winter months, businesses slowed down because I was in the northeast, and we provided outdoor grounds maintenance services and didn't do winter services.

Not only was I a full-time student and a business owner, but I was also a member of the basketball team. On weekends, if I did not have basketball practice or workouts, I would wake up at 4 a.m. to catch the SEPTA, which is Philly's public transportation rail system, to an Amtrak train from Philly to Harrisburg. I remember many times when I would come home, rush to get as much done as possible, and only jump onto the train as the door was closing.

I share stories like this with people when they see the "overnight success."

It's been many years of hard, hard work, and throughout the journey, I studied and worked to continue to improve my leadership.

Because it's a learned skill; it's learned leadership.

FIVE CRITICAL ELEMENTS OF LEADERSHIP[34]

One is **predicting**. Predicting is being able to recognize what's happening on the horizon, predicting the future. We do not

---

34   FWTX Staff, "Five Key Elements of Effective Leadership," *Fort Worth Magazine,* November 16, 2016.

have a crystal ball, we cannot see the future, but good leaders, with practice, begin to be able to pick up on enough signs that they can make pretty accurate reasonable predictions about their future. They don't get paralyzed by not having all the data. They can pick a path, and they work toward it.

Second is **simplification**. As businesses scale, changes happen. Leaders can keep things simple for their staff. There are so many things you can get caught up in, so stick to the fundamentals. When you hear people talk about mastery, it is getting good at those three or four things, not the three or four thousand things you need to do. If you simplify, it creates growth.

Third is **systematization**. Leaders look for opportunities to systematize and scale up at different levels. If you're a $1 million business and you're going to $3 million or $5 million at each one of these milestones, things have to change. Roles have to change, and yes, you may have to get out of the way as an owner or general manager. Your team may be able to do it better without you.

Fourth is **structure**. You have to have structure and know it will evolve. You have to know the capacities of people. Leadership is spending time to understand the structure and how it is changing.

Fifth is **delegation and elevation**. As you delegate, you elevate great leaders who can transfer responsibilities and have confidence they will be able to deliver the job.

If you are a 50 percent manager and 50 percent leader, that is fine, and whatever your ratio is, make sure you're spending time in these five areas. If you do, you will find that you're going to push and move your organization ahead. Fix the day-to-day—be somebody who solves the problem for good!

Now, as a leader. You've freed up time to continue to improve and drive the organization forward. Start with chapter one, follow the steps I've laid out in order, and this will ensure you are on the path to continued momentum.

MUSK CONTINUED

Elon Musk had an awareness of the need and saw what SpaceX could provide to the world. He calculated the return on the investment. He figured out how to reuse the same spaceship, put multiple people on, and transport people to make it affordable. He lowered the cost of space exploration by calculating the numbers.

He built a culture. In the *60 Minutes* interview, he described how many of the people who work on his team were some of the most qualified people across the globe who held high positions in the past. They chose SpaceX because they wanted to be a part of something great. They wanted to be a part of the organization that makes history.

SpaceX's culture is a part of the solution. It helps the strategy. Leadership is what Musk does best. It allows him to be the visionary: To dream, to create, to make it happen. To prove his doubters wrong.

The myth is momentum starts with leadership, because most people do not define leadership correctly when you connect all these.

You can send people out of this world to do things that people will never, ever think are possible in a short period.

FINAL THOUGHTS

The most successful organizations have strong leaders, not by force but by clear authority. These leaders own their decisions and empower their teams. Leaders focus on the future state of their industry and make the moves to be great, not good. Leadership is not always popular until they see your results.

CHAPTER 8

GET THE CROWD BEHIND YOU

———

"If you don't give the market the story to talk about, they'll define your brand's story for you."

—DAVID BRIER

"My favorite stories usually aren't from specific games or plays but from the interactions we've been blessed to have with players and our staff." This was Jay Wright's response when I asked him what stories or moments stood out during his career as a basketball coach.

"One example came last February at our final regular-season home game against St. John's. At halftime, we retired the jersey of Kyle Lowry. I was in the locker room with our team but catching up with Kyle and his family after the game was just amazing. To see his growth as a man to the husband and father he is today—not to mention an NBA champion and all-star—means a ton to me. And to watch the tape of the response he got from the Nova Nation really struck me."

Another example Jay brought up was around his staff.

"We've got a tremendous staff here, from coaches to graduate assistants to office people. It's really an underappreciated part of all this. This summer, we lost our office manager Helene Mercanti after a two-year battle with cancer. Helene did not share her diagnosis with many people when she received it. Only a few of us understood how ill she was. But her resilience and selflessness in showing up to work to do her job were incredible. It was a lesson for all of us. I think it impacted, and will continue to impact, each of us in this program."

People do not realize the power that internal stories have within organizations and how they connect people around a common mission. Often their power is overlooked, however, not with Villanova.

Under Jay's direction, Villanova won two men's national championships in 2016 and 2018. To put it in perspective, there are only two other active coaches who have won two or more National Championships, Mike Krzyzewski and Roy Williams.[35]

"All of us at Villanova benefit from an incredible tradition here. There have only been five head coaches here since 1936, and the four men who preceded me did incredible work

---

[35] Jacob Janower, "NCAA Tournament wins by coach: Most national championships in March Madness history," Sporting News, March 16, 2019.

building this foundation. That stretch started with Coach Alexander Severance, continued through Jack Kraft and Coach Mass, and then Steve Lappas in the 1990s. They were able to recruit great players and students who understood the mission of our university. We use the expression, 'We play for those who came before us,' and it's a cornerstone of our program. I think our current players have a good understanding of that connection. In more normal times, the former players are often around to watch practice or at our games. In the pandemic world, we use Zoom meetings to bring our basketball alums together. Our current guys have gotten to know their predecessors as more than just a name on a wall, and those interactions are a strength of our program."

The mission of the university is relayed to students and recruits through the stories of the past in conjunction with writing the story of the future. The special moments that are created fuel engagement.

Jay took me back to his start with Coach Rollie Massimino. "The biggest thing I had to learn as a young head coach was to be myself. I had worked for Coach Rollie Massimino as an assistant coach at Villanova and UNLV. I idolized Coach Mass. When I became head coach at Hofstra in 1994, I spent a good part of my first year trying to do things exactly the way Coach Mass had. But it didn't feel authentic to me or, I suspect, our players. I held on to the overriding principles I had learned from Coach Mass—treating the people in your program as a family, for one—but found that I had to do things in my own way. I couldn't be someone else, even if that someone else was a legend."

As Jay grew as a coach, he mentioned, "I learned that it's important to be a lifetime learner. As a coaching staff, we take a lot of care at the end of every season to self-evaluate. We look at what worked well and what things we can do better. That covers all aspects of our program, from technique to strategy to recruiting. We always try to be honest with ourselves about it. Both 2016 and 2018 were reminders of what I think is an essential truth at all levels of our game—you enjoy success when you have great players who are truly committed to your culture. We won in 2016 because we had Ryan Arcidiacono, Daniel Ochefu, Josh Hart, and Kris Jenkins. In 2018 we were led by Jalen Brunson, Mikal Bridges, Omari Spellman, Eric Paschall, Phil Booth, and Donte DiVincenzo. We were blessed with outstanding players who were invested in becoming the best young men and Villanova Basketball players they could be."

When I chose to get my Executive MBA at Villanova, I would be misleading you if I said I didn't buy into the story and tradition of the university. I was made aware of the university through the men's basketball's NCAA March Madness run. The more I looked into the university, the more its storied success stood out. The story was built over the years for both Jay and the university that would propel its organizational momentum.

When your internal story is genuine and gets amplified, it leads to explosive momentum. Winning the 2016 national championship didn't change anything at Villanova, it simply amplified its story, the story that has been told internally for years. It showed what Villanova University is and was before winning in 2016. As Villanova's story was highlighted through games and advertisements to the national audience, they saw applications spike. For the fall 2016 incoming class, Villanova received 17,266 applications. Following its 2016 national championship, applications rose to 21,095, a 21 percent increase.[36]

No doubt, the rise in applications came as a result of the increased publicity around the school during its tournament run. Villanova says it received more than thirty-five thousand media mentions from the start of the tournament through the title game and resulting victory parade. Those mentions included more than two hundred front-page mentions in newspapers nationwide the morning after its title win, including *The New York Times*, *The Wall Street Journal*, and *The Washington Post*.

According to studies commissioned by Butler University after its 2010 and 2011 appearances in the national title game, those media mentions are publicity money can't buy—at least probably more money than the universities have to spend.

The studies, completed by media firms Borschoff and Meltwater, found a combined publicity value of $1.2 billion for Butler during the 2010 and 2011 tournaments.[37]

"While I think our program's success benefits the university, it's also important to recognize the role the university plays in our program's progress. Under the leadership of [University President] Father Peter [Donohue, O.S.A.], our

---

36   Kristi Dosch, "Already, Loyola And Villanova Have Seen Benefits From Basketball Success," *Forbes*, June 25, 2018.

37   Ibid.

university has made incredible strides over the past fifteen years or so. That's true on the academic side as well as in the areas of endowment and campus development. We've seen that firsthand with the $65 million renovation that transformed the Finneran Pavilion from an aging building into a showpiece for Villanova Basketball. Through all of those advances, Villanova still very much retains the strong sense of community that is so important to our mission. It's really an awesome dynamic and an important part of our story."

When you understand the power of story, it connects, amplifies, and drives a deeper purpose to all those who hear it.

TEACHING THROUGH STORY

It was a hot summer afternoon at Wendy's. An older man, probably at least eighty years old, had just had lunch and walked out the door and started to walk toward his car.

Just as he opened the door to walk outside, torrential rain dropped from the sky, the kind of rain that looks like buckets, just dumping, hurricane-like.

The older man had a walker and decided to make a move for his car. Just as he was starting to get rained on, an umbrella covered him. A Wendy's employee had rushed out another door to grab one of their red picnic table umbrellas and held it over the man so he could stay dry and walk to his car.

This story is a fantastic example of an employee seeing the need to contribute in some way besides what is told to them. The principle is tough to teach, but when organizations can help their teams and staff to see "the need," it will leave an impact on people's lives. There is not a manual for this. No guide can truly teach you this, but the best way is through storytelling. If you think about that Wendy's employee, through that short story you can connect to the emotion of helping someone in need.

This is the art of storytelling. Storytelling is one of the secrets to get the crowd behind you!

I have shared this simple story many times with businesses to demonstrate what it takes to deliver exceptional customer service and get people on your side. How could you not cheer for this Wendy's employee and Wendy's as a whole? If you can train your people to see the need, it will change how your organization functions.

MISSING PIECE

Storytelling is the missing piece to amplify your message while connecting to your audience's own personal feelings and emotions. This works both for your staff and your customers. I discovered storytelling on my journey to becoming a speaker. I bought a course from Brian Tracey on public speaking. As I was watching it, he provided an outline to make a statement and follow it with a story that supports your statement. As I tried this with groups I spoke to, and even my team, I watched the rooms light up.

I remember going to speak to a group of college students at Penn State. It was a class in which the professor brings in speakers in the industry to share the real world with the students. It's very challenging to engage an audience for an extended period, especially an audience of nineteen-year-olds. I know when I was in their shoes, a guest speaker was just another person standing between me and whatever was happening on campus later. I decided I was going to incorporate stories into what I had to say. Actually, I decided to tell mostly all stories with a few other points to this tough crowd of college students.

I started with my story of leaving home at sixteen and how my stepdad was verbally abusive. I took them to the moment when he tried to stop me from succeeding. He came outside and told me that I could never use the lawnmower again. I showed them my struggle and how I was the laughingstock of the town with my outdated equipment. I shared my pride in doing good work and how I didn't care—maybe because I didn't know. I took them on the journey of how I got to where I am today. When I looked around the room, there was not one person with their head down. All eyes were on me, and I could see they were hooked. I knew if I could keep the attention of a college student for a whole period, there was something behind this "storytelling" thing.

INTEREST

The feeling of captivating an audience is addicting. After my Penn State experience, I wanted more. I started reading books on storytelling. I started with *Storyworthy* by Matthew Dicks.[38] From that book, I began to write down key moments in my days to not lose them. It was a way to capture them. Matthew Dicks

---

38   Matthew Dicks, *Storyworthy*, California: New World Library, 2018.

encourages you to use a simple spreadsheet and document the key moments in your life, because those are the stories that connect with people. When you start this, you think you don't have any stories until you realize stories are what make up life. The problem is most companies stop telling stories when they are trying to sell or build an audience, which prohibits their growth.

As I continued my journey to study storytelling, I came across the book *Stories That Stick* by Kindra Hall. In her book, she states, "Anytime you're in the middle of a mess, you're actually a story in the making. No matter how small the moment, if you craft it (the way she teaches) and match it to your message, you've got a possible story on your hands. It can be 'any happening or realization from your past. Any incident that happens on a Tuesday and makes you say, huh?' All of these are areas that can be crafted into a story." Kindra goes on to say, "Tell stories to get ahead. We are natural storytellers when we are with our friends or family but when it comes to business we freeze. We aren't encouraged to tell stories. Instead, we're encouraged to write reports, dig up facts, show our work, get the format right, and speak without umming." [39] When you understand storytelling and choose to leverage it, you will create explosive momentum by simply being you.

BE YOU! TELL YOUR STORY

One of my clients had a tragic event. John and his wife lost their son. Being a father, I cannot imagine the pain and heartache that this would cause.

---

39 Kindra Hall, *Stories That Stick,* (Tennessee: HarperCollins Leadership, 2019), page 199

As I was working with him, he came to me and said, "Seth, I'm not happy with my closing ratio."

I responded with, "Walk me through the flow of a meeting with your customer."

When he did this, I realized that he did not define his value as a business, which was something we worked on and fixed. But he also did nothing during the meeting to appeal to the customers' emotions. Let me be clear, this is not some magic trick or hypnosis, but the way humans connect. Disney and Pixar are media companies that have made billions on telling stories—stories that evoke emotion and response. When you understand the power of storytelling and the impact it has in business, you cannot avoid trying it.

I asked John what he was most passionate about. He told me, "When we lost our son, the community and everyone was so supportive. It was truly inspiring. My wife and I want to be able to give back to those in need. We want to fully fund a scholarship in our son's name."

I said, "Awesome. That is an amazing mission!" and I was inspired by the genuine desire to give back. I immediately followed, "We have to incorporate your story into your sales meeting!" That is exactly what we did.

Over the next couple of weeks, John started to work his story into his clients' meetings. At first, he said, "It felt weird, I fumbled it a bunch of times. I said too much to start, but once I practiced and made it simple, it was powerful." We worked to refine his story until it was clear and simple.

We then connected his value of being the least disruptive contractor, which became a huge hit with customers. Most of us have had a bad experience with a contractor and have felt the disruption in our lives. John crafted a story around a time that he saved a family from extreme disruption from a contractor. It made him different then everyone else they met with. He connected his story with real customer pain!

Next, John shared that the reason he works is to ultimately fund a scholarship in memory of his son. Most times the client wants to know more. This allows for a deeper level of personal conversation that 100 percent influences the sale. The best part of storytelling is you can use it to share your true mission and passion and show your customers or prospects that you are authentic. In John's situation, he just had to connect his mission and passion to his prospects. He was able to do this through storytelling.

John's closing ratio improved over 15 percent after implementing this technique! He went from closing 25 percent of his meetings to 40 percent. The only thing he did differently was connecting his value and mission to his passion through storytelling.

RIP-ROARING FIRE

I can remember as a kid going camping. As a family, we went camping one time a year. We did the tent thing. We didn't have a luxury camper or cabin. It was what they call primitive. One year, we rented a site with electricity, and that was a big deal! I'm not sure why anyone pays for that experience, but that was what our family camping trip entailed for years.

One of the years we went, we went for three days and it rained hard every day. It rained so hard we went to Walmart to get out of the rain for a few hours. Yes—with our wet dog. If you have a dog, you know what wet dog smells like. We came back with tarps and put them over our tents because our tents were leaking, but we still stayed.

On the last night, we had a short window of relief from the rain and decided to build our first campfire. Buying a five-dollar stack of dry wood was not in the budget, so we gathered wet sticks since it had been raining for days.

We worked to build a fire with wet sticks and struggled to get it going. We got it to catch eventually after we poured enough lighter fluid on the wet wood. (How we could afford lighter fluid but not wood, I'm not sure, and I don't advise this under any circumstance.)

By pouring the lighter fluid on it, we eventually got it hot, even using this damp wood. By adding fuel to the fire, it revved it up to a rip roaring fire. The rest of the wood that we put on that was damp dried out quickly and continued to burn.

My first five steps are the dry kindling in your life today, or in your business. Step six is the lighter fluid—storytelling. It will amplify your message. It will connect to your customers beyond any advertisement you can pay for.

You actually might have been picking up wet and damp kindling before this and are trying to start a rip-roaring fire. It can be done just like we did, but it is laborious. It symbolizes all the extra hours you have to put in, the energy it drains from you to get things working the right way, and the cash you may be short. Eventually, you make money, but it is hard, really hard.

What works best is if you use dry kindling as a starter. Think about how much faster your fire starts, burns, and burns hot.

Storytelling gets people behind you and makes everything easier. It makes that fire burn hotter, quicker, and more powerful. Storytelling is a way of connecting to the human side of life and telling stories that support the point you're trying to make. These stories speak to a person's heart. There are six key emotions: anger, disgust, fear, happiness, sadness, and surprise.

Think of a story that somebody told you that held onto your emotional chords. These stories stick with you just like John and losing his son and his passion to give back. It's inspirational.

You can retell a story much quicker than statistics and facts. Many people will remember a great story for years. Telling stories is one of the most potent ways that leaders can have influence. Stories teach, inspire, and make learning compelling. Storytelling makes connections between people and the ideas you are trying to convey.

Statistics show that roughly 40 percent of people are predominantly visual learners and learn the best from videos, diagrams, or illustrations. Another 40 percent are auditory learners. These people learn best through lectures and discussions. The remaining 20 percent are kinesthetic learners who learn best by doing, experiencing, or feeling with storytelling.[40] Storytelling incorporates all three types. Visual learners can appreciate the mental pictures that storytelling creates. Auditory learners focus on the words and the storyteller's tone and voice. Kinesthetic learners remember the emotional connections and what they felt from hearing the story.

Stories stick.

If I asked you to tell me about the Wendy's story, what happened, and what the point was, you would probably remember and be able to tell me.

A Wendy's employee saw the need and helped out an older man.

It's easily remembered along with the simple point of the story. It's short and effective. It has some of the six critical elements to a story that helps it connect to the listener.

Let's connect this to momentum. How is this putting fuel on the fire?

When you can tell a story that people get behind, it's like putting lighter fluid on the fire. It just revs it up. It takes it to a whole other level.

The problem with social media posts is that most lack a story. These posts do not connect with the audience. In stories that stick, Kindra highlights an Apple commercial.

---

40   Vanessa Boris," What Makes Storytelling So Effective for Learning?" *Harvard Business Publishing*, December 20, 2017.

It was shortly after Apple had a hiccup with importing the U2 album on everyone's phone.[41] Shortly after, they showed a commercial of a teenager always on their phone during holiday family time. It felt like he was being a checked-out teenager but at the end of the commercial, he captured all the special moments of their family time. Apple did not talk about features, styles, or how much memory the phone had. It told a story that everyone could connect to. It was memorable and easily retold to others. It stuck. When you post a story, something with a deep connection, or a narrative that somebody can follow, it speaks to people. They remember it; it will stick. I've run into people a year after I posted a story and it made such an impression that they brought it up in the conversation.

What was a key statistic I gave in this chapter? You probably don't remember. What was a key story I told in the chapter? You probably could tell at least one story to someone you know.

Stories make you twenty-two times more memorable.[42]

Some of the best speakers I've listened to have given the best talks with minimal facts and all stories. They would sprinkle in a statistic here and there, but they just told story after story after story when they were speaking.

I can remember just being connected, on the edge of my seat like a child listening for the next story, not for five

---

41   Kindra Hall, *Stories That Stick*, (Tennessee: Harper Collins Leadership, 2019), page 63

42   Kate Harrison, "A Good Presentation Is about Data and Story," *Forbes*, January 20, 2015.

minutes but an hour and fifty-five minutes. You stay engaged because it lights up a different part of your brain. Stories are memorable.

Statistics show that people are more likely to remember a **story** than a **statistic**… Only 5 percent of the listeners remembered a single **statistic**, while 63 percent remembered the **stories**. Research also shows that certain areas of our brains light up when we hear stories.[43]

THE PARTS OF A STORY BROKEN DOWN

The classic narrative arc is set in characters.

It is followed by tension and conflict.

There's a climax, or resolution, and a new norm.

If you want to get the crowd behind you, practice telling stories.

You will watch your audience be captivated by your stories. If you incorporate this into your business, you'll watch your team get behind you as they've never been behind you before. You will watch your customers follow you and want to do business with you. Finally, you will see your community support you and lift you up.

You will begin to experience how momentum makes everything easier.

---

43   Karen Friedman, "Primary Source: The Power of Storytelling in Business," *Public Relations Society of America, Inc.*, February 1, 2018.

FINAL THOUGHTS

Storytelling is the number one missing strategy for small- to medium-sized businesses. Storytelling will help you amplify your message, connect with customers, and improve your closing ratio. If you are not doing it, you must start. If you are doing it, invest time and energy into improving your natural presentation. You will crush your competition.

CHAPTER 9

MEASURE & ADJUST

"The ultimate purpose of collecting the data is to provide a basis for action or a recommendation."

—EDWARDS DEMING

"Your best isn't good enough! If you can't do better than your best, you're not going to make it on this team because you're going to kill us!"

These were the words of Nate Barton, former Blue Angel and flight trainer.

Imagine if you decided to commit to running your organization this way. Zero tolerance for error and 100 percent commitment to excellence. Your business would turn into a high-performing organization just like the Blue Angels.

When I first connected with Nate Barton, I wasn't exactly sure what he'd share. I knew the Blue Angels would have momentum, but I didn't know exactly where it would connect. I found it quickly as my conversation continued with Nate.

Nate Barton has been in the Navy for eighteen years. He ranks as a commander, and for him, being a part of the military aligned with sports because he was always a part of a sports team during high school and college. He grew up in a coaching family in which his dad Scott and mom Peggy both coached high school and college sports.

The Blue Angel pilots are the best of the best. The Blue Angels flight demonstration squadron was formed in 1946 by the US Navy. The unit is the second-oldest formal aerobatic team in the world. It is a representative sample of more than eight hundred thousand active-duty, reserve, and civilian men and women who serve throughout the Navy and Marine Corps, and upon completing their **Blue Angels** tours, they will return to the fleet to continue operational service.[44] About fifty of the highest-qualified pilots apply every year, while they only select two or three.

Nate continued to explain the process: "During my interview, it was intense. There were essays, strength tests, and about a week of social tests. All of the pilots have the skills, but they want to know that out of the aircraft you are a quality person. Even if you go to the grocery store and someone recognizes you, you have to be on. They want to know you are the person for the job. The lifestyle is on the road three hundred days a year, so you have to be able to clearly understand the requirements. We often would speak to Fortune 500 companies, NFL, and NBA teams. We've been involved with presidents, so character was paramount in the interview process."

---

44   United States Navy: Blue Angels Website, accessed September 4, 2020.

Many of his statements resembled Herb Magee's statements about building a team, order, and leadership. What continued to stand out during our conversation was the way the Blue Angels became and continue to stay a high-performance organization.

What separates the Blue Angels is the way it measures and adjusts almost every second. Consider this scenario: during a Chicago air show, over one million people were watching from the ground. Barton shared, "One of our pilots was out of position. Many people think the smoke [that comes out of the airplane] is for the fans; however, it is to tell the other pilots if they are out of position. The pilot is constantly measuring and adjusting to maintain position and if they find themselves slightly off, they then turn off their smoke as a signal and accountability measure. Trust is huge. You have to develop a trust for each other and it's a trust that can be taken away very easily. There were times it was definitely challenged."

In addition to the constant evaluation after each show, they would go into the film room and evaluate everything. Everything they did was filmed in high definition and would be evaluated, slowed down, and zoomed in—from the angle and speed of salute to a scuff on a boot. The level of accountability was in all the details way before they were in the air. "We definitely had some heated discussions, but we all became accustomed to accepting criticism and accepting when someone says that they screwed up," says Barton.

"One of these moments happened at our training facility in El Centro, California, home of the Blue Angels. There were two guys that I was training, and we were training on the 'Tuck under Break' maneuver. The Blue Angels don't fly it anymore because it was one of the most expensive maneuvers to fly. A pilot had to fly it hundreds and hundreds of times to figure it out. It was very difficult, and the crowd didn't think it was special. The first time we did it, we came close to three airplanes hitting each other. It was really bad. We ended up landing right away and debriefed and watched the film. As we watched the pilot make the critical mistake, I brought it up. When he told me, 'I'm doing my best,' I said 'Your best isn't good enough. If you can't do any better than that, you're not going to make this team because you're going to kill us.'"

That moment demonstrates the power of measuring performance, holding people accountable, and adjusting. In building this team, it was crucial to find people that would be able to handle the culture of constructive criticism. But this is what drives consistent organizational excellence and momentum. Our team recognized we had to remove our ego from the room," Barton shared. "I want to hear everything I did wrong from your perspective so I can fix it. I gained your trust and you gained mine so we both knew we wanted to make the team as good as possible. We had the same ultimate goal. Call me out when I do something, but better yet, I want to be able to call myself out."

Organizations get sloppy with holding their teams accountable because most times it's not life or death. They allow mistakes to be made and poor service to be delivered because maybe they don't want to offend anyone. In order to build a winning organization that continues to win, it is important that you have a way to measure, discuss, improve, and then adjust as you go. Training and preparing are also critical elements to consider. Nate said, "We have to do some maneuvers one thousand, maybe two thousand times before we do it in an airshow."

Imagine if you invested in the preparation and training first and then continued to look to improve every day. Measuring and adjusting is the last step of the momentum process because when you do this with the same intensity, and you follow the previous six steps, you will have ongoing momentum forever because you stay fluid, flexible, and focused.

IT'S LIKE A FINE WINE

If they say you can't do it... that means you probably should.

That is how Marty Schoffstall and Rebecca Kline felt when they started Spring Gate Vineyard in 2014. Spring Gate is located on sixty acres that Marty Schoffstall owns and is now one of the largest vineyards in Pennsylvania. Rebecca was there from the beginning. Her background was in tax and finance, and she originally worked with Marty for some of his other business ventures in years prior. In 2010, she helped plant the first grapes, four years before they would have their first tasting. Everyone told them no, and everything seemed to be against them: the soil, the climate, the topography and township, and even the myth of following the wine industry protocol and rating systems. They basically said in order to have good wine, you have to go to shows and get rated by a "judge."

"The wine industry was stuck in old ways. Old ways are not always bad, but they weren't open to change the way you make a merlot. They told you how a merlot should taste. The same for a chardonnay. They would tell winemakers the characteristics and had a strict and regimented protocol to be considered good. We were competing against California wines, Napa Valley, etc., but we realized that our customers did not want a Napa Valley experience in Central Pennsylvania. We took a disruptive approach and decided we were going to use hybrid grapes that do better in cooler climates. We also developed a base wine that we could adapt to different blends. Our focus in all of this was to make a wine that our customers said was the best. We made a commitment to not go to shows and we didn't really care about judging. Our customers were the judges. We allowed the customers to make requests, and we measured the success of products and adjusted quickly. We found out that the people in Central Pennsylvania really enjoy sweet wines, including sparkling wines. When people think of sparkling wines, they think of champagne, but we found people really enjoyed the change.

"The next thing that we focused on was the guest experience. We wanted people to come to Spring Gate because they have a good experience. The wine really only complements the experience. The wine just can't be bad. Our first weekend, we had fifty people show up. We couldn't believe it. The next weekend was two hundred, and today at our festivals, we have over three thousand people at times. This success continued because we kept measuring what we were doing and quickly adjusted. We looked at who was coming and why they were coming. We evaluated the times of year we had different events and the turnouts."

Kline continues, "We realized women were our largest client at the time. When we realized that they were coming in one time per month, we worked on a plan to get them in two times in a month, maybe three. We noticed their husbands were not coming, so we wanted to get them to come along. The men were not into 'wine slushies.' We thought men would come if we had beer, so we started a brewery. We were constantly looking at what was working and pivoting to what worked better. Now we had the whole family coming multiple times per month, which continued to grow our business. We have been in growth mode since the day we opened our doors."

Their measure and adjust method worked to help them successfully navigate the pandemic. "Even when COVID hit, we tried things quickly, measured their success, and adjusted. One of the things that we tried was home delivery. We quickly adapted that into neighborhood deliveries. Neighborhood deliveries turned into adding a food truck. It allowed people to connect with their neighbors while socially distancing and building community during a challenging time. By continually evaluating what we are doing, we have been quick to adjust, and it has continued to fuel our momentum even in the most challenging situations, like COVID, when we had to be shut down for visitors coming to us."

Spring Gate is an amazing example of how to continue to measure and adjust. By continuing to do this, they have kept sustainable momentum. According to Daniel Newman, Thomas Edison designed thousands of light bulb prototypes before he created one that could actually be used by the masses. Imagine if he had thrown in the towel after his first ten attempts? Or his first one thousand? Well, over 125 years later, business is starting to recognize the method to Edison's madness: failing fast to create lasting innovation.[45]

45 Daniel Newman, "Secret to Digital Transformation Success: Fail Fast to Innovate Faster," *Forbes,* May 16, 2017.

THE IMPORTANCE OF SCORE

Imagine five minutes before the Super Bowl. Your favorite team is actually in the Super Bowl this year, and they have a great chance at winning. They haven't won in over thirty years, and you've been a fan your whole life. Five minutes before the game, they announced that they're not going to keep score. They don't want to hurt anybody's feelings. And they really don't want to have a loser. They just want to play to play the game and enjoy the game but not keep score.

How would you feel? Some of the feelings that you may experience are disappointment, frustration, and maybe even anger.

It would be natural to feel these emotions if there's such an abrupt change.

What changed? The players are still the same. The coaches are still the same, and there are still people in the stands. There are people still watching it. But why did you lose excitement? Why did the energy shift? Why is keeping score so important? Keeping score is a measurement of how to win, how to succeed. And there's something connected to it in our nature.

We have a desire to keep score to measure who is winning. Who is the better team?

Let's examine two games—a close game, and a blowout game. I can remember the 2005 college football national championship. It featured Vince Young of the University of Texas and Reggie Bush of the University of Southern California (USC). The game was dynamic and so close it came down to the final play. I can remember being in the basement of an old dormitory at Wyoming Seminary Prep School sitting on an old blue box seat. My whole experience and senses were heightened because of the excitement of the game. Texas would take the lead and then USC would come back. It was one of my favorite college football games to date.

Another great example of similar excitement is the Kentucky Derby. As the lead horse changes frequently it creates excitement; with only a few seconds of lightning speed separating the victor from defeat. As the jockeys are on those horses, the measurement is their position, the adjustment is the jockey's responsibility with the horse. During the whole race, the jockey evaluates whether they're inside, against the rail, or outside... if they need to save the horse's energy from the start, the middle, or the end. As people watch, the announcers feed into the excitement of who is in the lead each second. Without being able to measure who is winning, the race would not be as impactful.

This energy is very similar to driving success in organizations. Your staff, team, and organization become more engaged in all areas when they know the score.

Score is a form of measurement. Based on the score, teams and organizations make adjustments and try to improve just like the jockey example. If a team is losing at halftime, their coaches review all the stats, their passing yards, their running yards, how the defense has been performing, and then they make adjustments. They review which players are the weak links and which players have an advantage based on what they are seeing. For the best organizations and companies or sports teams, when they're leading, they're still making adjustments, they're still measuring the stats. Even if you go into halftime with the lead, you continue to make adjustments. Bill Belichick of the New England Patriots was one of the best. The team's streak started in 2002. As of 2015, it was seventy-four to zero at home when leading at halftime—the same way the jockey who is in the front of the whole pack is not going to stop making adjustments on the horse.[46]

Organizations keep score through their financial statements. This includes profit and loss, balance sheet, customer retention, and sales account management. Key performance indicators can be used to keep score. It's important to simplify them and know what really keeps your momentum going.

Here are a couple of companies that rose quickly but failed to measure and adjust and ultimately went out of business or had significant challenges.

Borders—It was a book retailer. It had stores all over. But it wasn't able to adapt to all the technological changes in the 2000s. Many of its customers were switching to digital versions of books, and Borders actually focused on growing its DVD and CD departments. It kept building, but it didn't invest in the digital footprint, an online presence, or a plan. Believe it or not, it actually even outsourced some of its online sales to Amazon. By September 2011, all of its stores were shut down.[47]

---

46   "Patriots Are Now 74-0 When Leading at Halftime at home in the Regular Season since 2002," Reddit, 2016.

47   Jennifer Guerra, "Borders Closing Its Bookstores After 40 Years," *NPR: Public Broadcasting,* July 19, 2011.

By comparison in a similar market, Amazon started out selling books. It continued to measure what the customers were looking for, looked at what the future held, and made adjustments.

If we evaluate Borders through my seven-step process, Borders lacked the awareness of what was happening in the market. Awareness and mindset are where it starts. Borders did not understand the return on the investment and the value of moving to the online space. It saw value in the book, DVD, and CD market, which proved to be its downfall. Even if it had a great culture, it missed the mark on the two essential pieces.

I was speaking to a group, and two members were debating which was more important to start with. One of the members said culture and the other said leadership. I think they missed the whole momentum talk, but I helped point out that Borders could have had the greatest culture in the world, but because it lacked awareness of their team, leaders, and/or the market, it still found itself out of business.

Another great example of what happens when you do not measure and adjust is Toys "R" Us. Toys "R" Us used to be the go-to spot for all toys, from babies on up through a child's life, Toys "R" Us was it. It had a niche market and controlled it.

As stores like Target, Walmart, and Amazon started to enter the market, it wasn't measuring, and if it was, it did not adjust to the way the market was changing.

Organizations either get a flat tire here or continue to roll like Spring Gate.

KEEP ROLLING

The momentum meter (see chapter "How to use Momentum Meter") is a tool that helps you keep rolling. When you are actively measuring and adjusting you realize you may need to change. You may realize that the market is changing. Your hand may be forced to change because of circumstances outside of your control like the coronavirus.

The way the momentum meter is designed is you flow right back into awareness. For Borders or Toys "R" US, they should have dived back into step one, awareness and mindset. For Blockbuster, it could have been its limiting belief that late charges were a good thing and a significant part of its revenue. Spring Gate continues to adjust its long-term vision and monitor the hidden value/costs from step three.

Next comes fixing any company culture issues and getting your team engaged in strategy.

If you are a leader at this point, leadership becomes much easier, and you can focus on the future versus the day-to-day. Finally, amplify your message and spread it to the world, or your market!

The best teams and organizations measure their success so they can see that they're winning and they're still making adjustments, which connects very closely to awareness.

The momentum meter, when followed, will keep your momentum ongoing forever!

OTHER NOTABLE COMPANIES THAT FAILED TO ADJUST[48]

- Compaq
- Oldsmobile
- Howard Johnson
- Kodak
- Sears
- AOL

COMPANIES THAT TURNED AROUND

Apple has one of the most impressive turnaround stories. Apple is one of the most valuable companies in the world. But there was a time when it was actually about to be bankrupt.

A little over twenty years ago, they were losing about a billion dollars a year.[49]

That's when Steve Jobs returned and launched products like the Mac and iPod.

And now Apple products have a whole new brand identity for being the latest in technology. They became premium.

It's easy to measure when you're losing.

Because you can feel the pain, and change happens when pain is strong enough.

---

48 Katie Nolan, "9 Iconic American Brands That No Longer Exist," Bob Vila: Action Media, Inc., accessed September 21, 2020.

49 Avery Hartmans and Matt Weinberger, "Steve Jobs Would Have Been 65 on Monday," *Business Insider*, February 24, 2020.

But they adjusted. Steve Jobs knew an adjustment had to be made; Apple had to do things differently. At that point, he dove back into the awareness and calculated his ROI and value of what he could bring, and the rest fell in place.

Best Buy is another great example that made changes, unlike organizations such as Circuit City, which went out of business.

Starbucks struggled during the financial crisis of 2008.[50] Unlike a lot of other companies, it actually did not require government intervention. But it was so bad that Howard Schultz came back in to get things straight. The company grew so quickly that it was struggling from its fast growth. Schultz quickly set out to change things, and he invited a lot of open feedback. He was measuring what was going on. He was getting feedback. That's another form of measurement. He was able to adjust the plan. He closed some locations. It rebranded some of its advertising campaigns, and it got serious about social media. And it emerged stronger than ever.

AMAZON

Amazon started out with books and invested in data technology and customer experience. Amazon is valued at over a trillion dollars today. But how it got there was through building a culture of metrics.

Amazon's culture of metrics started as a common theme throughout its growth and development: its desire to use a

---

50   Husain, Khan and Mirza, "Brewing Innovation," *Business Today,* September 28, 2014.

measured approach on all aspects of its business, not just in its financials, but everywhere.

One of its employees in 2004 described one of its corporate boot camp meetings in January 1997, when the Amazon CEO Jeff Bezos, "saw the light." While addressing much of his senior staff, he said at Amazon there is a culture of metrics. He went on to explain how being a web-based business gave Amazon an amazing insight into how humans behaved. Amazon recorded every move a visitor made: every click and movement of the mouse. It compiled massive amounts of data, broke it down, and looked at it from the flow of click-throughs after the purchase. It wanted to measure customer enjoyment.

One member of the team said, "We can do that by tracking the time they spend on our site."

"Not specific enough," Jeff Bezos said.

"How about the average number of minutes each customer spends on the site per session?" another member shouted out.[51] If that goes up, they must be having a blast."

Amazon dove deep into all areas to understand what its customers liked and enjoyed and if it was getting beneficial measurement. It invested heavily in its shopping cart. It changed the shape, style, and color, as well as the location. Did the top left work better than the top right? Hundreds of questions

---

51   Dave Chaffey, "Amazon.com marketing strategy: A business case study," Smart Insights, October 14, 2020.

were considered to perfect the optimal location. It measured sales and adjusted accordingly.

It tracked pixels and cookies to be able to retarget items that a customer looked at or show similar items

Some people view it as an infringement on their privacy. Others view it as helpful. If I buy a product and there's a complementary product that will make my life easier, I'm happy Amazon shows me the option. It is still my choice to buy it. I remember being in class at Villanova and one of my professors decided to see how smart Amazon really was. He put in all his data, information, and preferences as he viewed items. The main item he was looking for was a new Jeep. As he viewed Jeeps before he bought one, Amazon was tracking his every move. After he purchased his Jeep, Amazon tried to sell him tires. His conclusion was that if Amazon was as smart as people give it credit for, it would have known that he didn't need tires when he just purchased a new vehicle. Even if it doesn't get it right every time, the data it uses helps it adjust to the client's preferences, which helps drive sales.

Amazon has been exceptional at being able to adjust and look ahead to the future, which connects closely to awareness. It understands what happened to many of the other companies like Borders, Blockbuster, AOL, and Sears just to rename a few.

FINAL THOUGHTS

Measuring what you are doing and adjusting will keep your momentum going forever. It is a simple message, but people forget its importance. The momentum meter is a simple tool that I created that will help you take a holistic view of the seven most important gauges to starting and sustaining momentum. Make it a weekly or monthly check-in, and you will continue momentum forever.

CHAPTER 10

CONCLUSION

———

"The whole is greater than the sum of its parts."

—ARISTOTLE

KETO

I'm not one to do a "fad" diet. I've never done one. I always just try to watch what I eat and maintain a balanced diet. I exercise three to five times a week from basketball, biking, running, or weight training.

One summer day during the coronavirus pandemic. I stopped by my friend Matt Owens' house. It was early in the year, and we didn't know much about it at the time. As I talked to Matt, he told me he did keto and it changed his life. "Seth, I haven't slept through the night in fifteen years. Since I've been on keto, I'm sleeping through the night. I have more energy, and I feel like I'm twenty-five again." (Matt is in his early fifties.)

He looked great and his enthusiasm sold me on trying it. Up until the pandemic, I played basketball two times per week, as well as a pickup league or two. When the pandemic hit, all activity slowed down. I felt like I was going to add a few extra pounds in quarantine.

The keto diet eliminates or significantly reduces sugar and carbohydrates. In the 1980s, the American Heart Association came out with the theory that fats were unhealthy and removed them from many of the foods.[52] They advertised "low-fat," and as they removed the fat, they had to replace it with something for flavor. They replaced the fats with carbohydrates. Fat and proteins are essentials for the body to function properly. Carbohydrates are not essential for the body to function.[53] When you eliminate sugars and carbs, your body goes into ketosis. The liver produces ketones, and your body switches to run on protein and fat versus carbs and sugar.

As I started keto, I really didn't think anything would be different. I did immediately notice that the food tasted way better. Adding fat back into your diet really was enjoyable. My wife loves to cook, so we were having some of our best meals on this "diet." It didn't make sense. This was supposed to be wrong. Over the next two months, I stuck to the keto plan pretty strictly. I took in less than fifty carbohydrates per day and eliminated almost all sugar. In two months, I lost twenty-five pounds and was back to my high school weight while eating a tasty diet.

---

52 Mark Hyman, *Fat Fiction*, Prime Video, 2020.

53 Kris Gunnars "Good Carbs, Bad Carbs — How to Make the Right Choices," *Healthline*, August 18, 2016.

Now I was curious. How could I have missed this? I continued to investigate and came across the movie *Fat Fiction* on Prime. *Fat Fiction* addresses this myth about carbohydrates and their benefits. It really sunk in when I saw a picture of Times Square in the seventies and then in 2018. Everything was basically the same except for the weight of the people. In the seventies, everyone was skinny and in shape, and fifty years later, everyone is about fifty to one hundred pounds heavier. In 1980, when the American Heart Association announced this new dietary recommendation, people followed it.[54] Food makers adjusted, and the result can be seen by looking at the weight gain as well as those with type 2 diabetes since 1980.

How can it be that by eating fat, I lost fat? It didn't make sense.

BUSINESS AND KETO

The business world is very similar to my keto experience. Many of us are told what is important to succeed in business. Some of us have been told it's culture. Some of us have been told it's leadership. For some, they believe a great strategy will connect you to the dreams and promise of being a business owner. The life of abundance and freedom. For most business owners, it's a joke now, and they don't see a way. I'm here to say that many have been wrong and have put too much weight on one area and missed the holistic approach.

I'm here to let you know that you can believe in the dreams of being a business owner. You can have a life of abundance, and it can be better than you imagine.

---

54 Mark Hyman, *Fat Fiction*, Prime Video, 2020.

It's not your fault, just like the people who believed low-fat and carbohydrates are good for you. When I got the right recipe for my diet, I lost more weight faster than I have ever done before. The craziest part: it was easy.

My seven steps to momentum are easy. They are clear and will lead to significant gains in your business. I'm asking you to try them. Try them with all your might, power, and resources. You will become an advocate of momentum and its power. The best part is once you know the recipe and its ingredients, it becomes easier and easier to make. And trust me... the only thing that is going to get fat is your wallet and bank account.

TRUST THE PROCESS

Throughout the book, I provided examples of where companies and leaders have used my elements of momentum. The ones that have had the most success and continue to succeed are using all seven elements, even if they call them something different. My seven steps are set up to help you understand the process of starting and sustaining momentum. When you complete them in this order, you will continue to have sustained momentum. Most companies can start momentum, but the challenge to sustain it is where they falter. Below is a summary of the seven steps.

THE 7 STEPS SUMMARIZED

AWARENESS/MINDSET:

First, you must evaluate your awareness. What are your limiting beliefs? What is holding you back that you may not realize? Your mindset is your foundation for the success of your organization. If you mess this step up, any other step you start with will provide short-term momentum. This step will feel awkward at first, and you will want to dive into more strategy, but the more time you spend in this step, the bigger your impact will be.

VALUE/ROI:
After you understand your mindset and limiting beliefs and dive to understand current awareness, it's time to evaluate value. Value has three components:

- The value you offer and what differentiates you as a company—most companies miss the deep dive

- Hidden value and costs in your organization—ones that do not directly show up on financial statements

- Calculate the return of your proposed effort or energy

CULTURE:
At this point, you will evaluate your existing culture and fix any issues prior to launching any new initiatives. You will also see if you have been recruiting the correct team members or you need to make adjustments. Once you evaluate your existing culture, you will bring your team in on the thoughts of what you found from your deep dive. You want to add their ideas and get their buy-in to the process. You will feel like you may want to start here, but you will not know what evolved from some of your deep dives in the prior two steps that will accelerate your team. Trust me.

STRATEGY:

Here is where you will involve your team in discussion and have them help craft a plan for the initiatives that you uncovered. You should have a clear picture of hidden costs and areas of value, and by this point, you will understand any mindset challenges that are having an impact. All of this will be considered for the initiative you are working toward. It is important to define how you are going to measure your strategy and who is accountable for what. The power of your team will be showcased here to help build a solution that works. They will add to what you already discovered, and you will have more concrete numbers to share.

LEADERSHIP:

Your role as a leader is to help make sure you are gauging these elements up until this point. Yes, you have been leading throughout the process, however, now is the time to continue to look toward the future. You have engaged and set up your team in a way that they can do the work. You should have a clear strategy and assigned roles that your managers keep in check. Your time will become freer, and you will have the ability to continue to give direction that leaves an impact on your organization. At this point, you should begin to feel the shift between a manager and leader happening.

GET THE CROWD BEHIND YOU:

When you have the first five steps completed and running well, it is time to amplify your message. It is time to get a larger audience and start feeling the force of momentum. When you are aligned in this way, you will start connecting stories to your mission, work, and life. You will see an explosion in your organization if you consistently commit to storytelling. The crowd will follow you, it will support you, and it will push you to new heights!

MEASURE AND ADJUST:
Consistently measure against your key performance indicators or desired results and adjust sooner rather than later if you see a trend. First, you have to have something to measure, which you should have set up during the strategy step, but then you have to adjust based on what you see. When something in the market, your team, or plan needs adjustment, you go back to step one in awareness/mindset. As you run through the process again, it will help evaluate the impacts of changing or not and will ultimately help you create another strategy that you can measure and adjust to.

The more you go through these steps, the easier they will get, and your momentum will increase exponentially.

THE SAVINGS OF SPEED

Whether you are a contractor, a business owner, or a leader, you know that when you save time, it equals money. My momentum process is very simple, and at first glance, it may look easy to do by yourself. I would encourage you to connect with me and my team to talk about solutions for your organization. My Momentum U program teaches all of these principles in a custom plan with your organization. I have watched countless people get a tenfold return in eight weeks. Just like my keto diet, when you have the right recipe, results happen quickly!

HOW TO USE THE MOMENTUM METER

———

"Order and simplification are the first steps toward the mastery of a subject."

—THOMAS MANN

The momentum meter is a tool I designed to be able to help start momentum, but more importantly, sustain it. When used properly, it will help keep your momentum going forever. The tool is used to help show you gaps and where you need to put your focus to ensure you maintain sustainable momentum.

HOW TO START

First, make sure you read each chapter and have an understanding of each step to build momentum. If you have questions, refer back to some of the concepts that are covered in the
chapters. Once you understand each momentum component,
gauge yourself from one to five on that topic on where you
think you fall based on your current state. Once you score
a four out of five, you can move to the next gauge/step. For
example, evaluate yourself from one to five on the topic of
awareness/mindset. I would recommend having an outside
perspective to help initially, especially on the awareness/
mindset. This area is the foundation of momentum, so it is
essential to build this foundation correctly

1) Awareness/ Mindset: Rate yourself a five if...

- You have done a deep dive on yourself and have identified your blind spots.

- You have examined your narrative and understand your limiting beliefs.

- You understand and define the current and future state of your industry.

- You understand and commit to working on awareness/ mindset ongoing, as it is the foundation of momentum.

2) Value: Rate yourself a five if...

- You have identified and put a numerical value on hidden costs.

- You evaluated impact/ ROI (in dollars) of taking new courses of action.

- You clarified your company value.

3) Culture: Rate yourself a five if...

- Your current culture is how you want it to be or how you intend. Remember some organizations have a fast-demanding culture, and it works. Some want a family-friendly culture. It is your choice, but examine it. You must recruit people who desire that culture, or it will not be in alignment.

- Do not move to the next step until your culture is four out of five.

4) Strategy: Rate yourself a five if…

- Your current strategy has been working.

- Your new strategy is through the lens of your new awareness/mindset and the three value points, and you built this new strategy with your team involved and created key performance indicators to measure your new plan.

5) Leadership: Rate yourself a five if…

- You are holding your managers accountable to the strategy that was laid out.

- You are keeping a pulse on all the five—soon to be seven—momentum gauges. When you see they are below a four, you are taking action.

- You are spending time working toward the future state of your organization.

6) Energy / Amplify: Rate yourself a five if…

- You have developed compelling stories that align with your organization's newfound success.

- You are incorporating storytelling into recruiting, sales, management, fundraising, investing, etc.

7) Measure and Adjust: Rate yourself a 5 if...

- You are regularly checking the gauges and working to keep them at or above a four out of five.

If adjustment is needed, start at awareness and mindset and make sure your foundation is correct, and then continue through the remaining steps/gauges.

ACKNOWLEDGMENTS

I never imagined I would become a published author. It is one of my prized professional accomplishments. The journey was long and hard but inspiring. I met so many great people along the way. I want to thank everyone who contributed in some way to my life over the years. It includes all of you—the good and the bad. All of it has made me who I am. I am here because of you. A special thanks to Dan and Barbara Eichenlaub and Gern Haldeman for seeing the potential in me and believing in me even in my hardest moments. I owe you the world.

To my family, I love you. To my wife Janelle, thank you for your support for my countless business endeavors and passion for continual improvement. You are always by my side, and I cannot thank you enough. To our beautiful daughter Brooke, I'm enjoying every minute of your growth and can't wait to be alongside you every step of the way.

To my grandparents, Herman and Kathryn, who are looking down; you helped give me the foundation as a kid to make it to where I'm at.

To my mom, thank you for your consistent unwavering support. I don't say it enough, but I love you.

To my brothers: Jaric, one of my proudest moments has been able to work with you for over fifteen years. You have been with me on my business journey. Janard, you have grown into a special man. I am proud of you both.

To Cory, Lisa, Arielle, and Angelica: I am so thankful we met and you have accepted me into your family

Thank you to Eric Koester for the opportunity to write my book. Thank you to Travis Wright for the introduction and to my editors Jacqueline Claire Reineri Calamia, Christy Mossburg, Brian Bies, and the rest of the team at New Degree Press that played a role in the process. To Brandon Grumbine, my general manager, leadership staff, and my assistant Taylor Grabiak. It takes a village!

And thank you to everyone who gave me their time for a personal interview, preordered the ebook, paperback, and multiple copies to make publishing possible, helped spread the word for *Momentum: Where Mindset Meets Strategy: Seven Steps to Start and Keep Momentum in Business Forever* to gather amazing momentum, and helped me publish a book I am proud of. I am sincerely grateful for all of your help.

PERSONAL INTERVIEWS

Joe Foster	Herb Magee
Jay Wright	Taylor Bryant
Rebecca Kline	Nikki Katsaounis
Bill Simpson	Shane Woodman
Jordan Norwood	John Fecile
Dr. Stephen Klasko	Geeta Nadkarni
Ernie Accorsi	Nate Barton

PRE-SALE SUPPORTERS

Joy Karsner	Joi Notice-Brooks
Marissa Hoover	Catie Gingrich
Brandon Grumbine	Patricia Freudenberg
Brandon Conway	Scott Riegel
Bill Simpson*~	Ashley Kranick
Nina Reese	Tracy Petrovich*
Mario Goldsby	Jay Megonnell
Moe Martin	Rob Breakiron
Kristen Hazel	Kevin Go
Kyle Flanagan	John Poe
Eric Moyer	Colleen Arnold
Brad Goss	Brad Wetzel
Shane Woodman~	Chris Zaucha
Josh Gregor	Ann Chikowski
Malcolm Ingram*	Taylor Bryant
Melissa Schaeffer	Jory Barrad

Roy Schutzengel

Jordan Gregor

Al Pizzica

Mike O'Malley

Eric Koester

Mike Schreiner

Melissa Bassano

Jeff Kemmerer

Jordan Wartman

Jen Zajac*

Anthony Penna

Chad Cohle

Hayden Mclaughlin

Stan Phelps

Paul Gaspich

Kory Beidler

Frank Collins

Cory Laws*

Stephen Mosser

Dave Heinrich

Kristina Wolfe

Aaron Buchman

Jeff Sider

Garrett Shumaker

Frank Brescia

Ryan Bowe

Justin Kemmerer

Erin Pizzeck

Luke Olenoski

Jessica White*

Scott Lesak*

Beth Walters

KerriLaine Prunella

Kevin Kindig

Jon Gross

Amit Chahwala

Sean Woodman

Dave Gallagher*

Rebecca Kline~

Tom Pomanti

Mandi Mease

Scott Barton

Luke Hanmer

Dan Hodge*

Nicole Loser

Chase Paterno*

Ray Farrell

KD Patel

Alfred Sloan

Mike Schweigler

Karthik Mohan

Luke Henry*

Brooke Reynolds

Toni & TC Clark*

Pam Hartnett*

Jonathan Winder

Zach Bleiler

Trenton Petrovich

Bob & Lori Bourque*

Jared Motter

Jared Armstrong

Pierre Scott

Geoffrey Crout

Russ Frederick

Tara Cooley

Katherine Noss

Art Miller*

James Szivos

Janet Megonnell

Kristi Horner

Fred Rodgers

Adam Malavé

Ben Gearhart

Tom Smith

Matteo Zullo

Bill Cowen

Ken Carpenter*

Claire Bruno*

Tristan Crawford

Aaron Hall

Steven Spieker

Todd & Deb Garber

Andrea Hood

William Wilson

Jeffrey Kudisch*

Janelle Lewis

Peter Darlington

Brian Arcaro

Aaron Bryant

Ahmet Sari

Shanika Cooper

Tim Wartinbee

Ken Parker

Cady North

Steve Kindler

Matt Mitchell

John Skitka

Rachel Hersh*

David Frees

Rob Klock

Matt Malone

Dan Eichenlaub

APPENDIX

INTRODUCTION

"The 60 Minutes Interview: Southwest's Herb Kelleher." *60 Minutes Rewind.* January 4, 2019. video, 11:01. https://www.youtube.com/watch?v=MyiI8FoJk54.

"Southwest Airlines Reports 47th Consecutive Year of Profitability." *Investor Relations.* Southwest Airlines Co. January 23, 2020. http://investors.southwest.com/news-and-events/news-relea ses/2020/01-23-2020-112908345.

CHAPTER 1

Mawer, Rudy. "10 Signs and Symptoms That You're in Ketosis." *Healthline,* August 2, 2018. https://www.healthline.com/nutrition/10-signs-and-symptoms-of-ketosis.

Taylor, Jane. "What Are Your Biggest Limiting Beliefs?" *Jane's Journal* (blog). Accessed March 16, 2020. https://www.habitsforwellbeing.com/what-are-your-biggest-limiting-beliefs/.

CHAPTER 2

"AMA CEO Russ Klein Talks about the Gift of Mentorship." AMA Toronto. October 10, 2019. video, 1:03. https://www.youtube.com/watch?v=NEw7-8UB_Ew.

Borysenko, Karlyn. "How Much Are Your Disengaged Employees Costing You?" *Forbes.* May 2, 2019. https://www.forbes.com/sites/karlynborysenko/2019/05/02/how-much-are-your-disengaged-employees-costing-you/#35367e183437.

Comaford, Christine. "76% of People Think Mentors Are Important, but Only 37% Have One." *Forbes.* July 3, 2019. https://www.forbes.com/sites/christinecomaford/2019/07/03/new-study-76-of-people-think-mentors-are-important-but-only-37-have-one/#4c0ac00f4329.

Entrepreneur Encyclopedia. s.v. "Return on Investment." Entrepreneur Media. Accessed March 18, 2020. https://www.entrepreneur.com/encyclopedia/return-on-investment-roi.

Harrison, Kate. "New Study Reveals Entrepreneurs Need More Mentoring." *Forbes*. October 30, 2018. https://www.forbes.com/sites/kateharrison/2018/10/30/new-study-reveals-entrepreneurs-need-more-mentoring/#3c86d0ff7819.

Macrotrends. "Netflix Revenue 2006-2020." Accessed March 25, 2020. https://www.macrotrends.net/stocks/charts/NFLX/netflix/revenue.

Merriam-Webster. s.v. "value (n.)." Accessed March 18, 2020. https://www.merriam-webster.com/dictionary/value.

Morris, Rhett. "Mentors Are the Secret Weapons of Successful Startups." *TechCrunch*. March 22, 2015. https://techcrunch.com/2015/03/22/mentors-are-the-secret-weapons-of-successful-startups.

Netflix, Inc. (NFLX). NasdaqGS - NasdaqGS Real-Time Price. Accessed March 25, 2020. https://finance.yahoo.com/quote/NFLX/key-statistics/?guccounter=1&guce_referrer=aHRocHM6Ly93d3cuZ29vZ2xlLmNvbS88&guce_referrer_sig=AQAAAAYlD-YEInE5PAOHVOBTScZuUN-jWjUPUEBJyLdxmgJRrzAPIf1BBa3sW8TJPn-6l_NhMb5hYY8XWGkqYDxPotEoDyI7yZlTRzNLrcBPVOlxyQDtPY4iYSEu2ej3cJDjwt-Pmj6IjjfZsxFaMNibcceDiiG7uhXMjmoP1olwP_ify.

Olito, Frank. "The Rise and Fall of Blockbuster." *Business Insider*. August 20, 2020. https://www.businessinsider.com/rise-and-fall-of-blockbuster.

Rampton, John. "How a Mentor Can Increase the Success of Your Business." *Inc*. October 1, 2020. https://www.inc.com/theupsstore/how-the-ups-store-redesign-is-helping-small-businesses-grow.html.

RAMSEY. "Return on Investment; the 12% Reality." Accessed March 18, 2020. https://www.daveramsey.com/blog/the-12-reality#:~:text=The%20S%26P%20500%20gauges%20othe.

CHAPTER 3

"Sportswear Maker Adidas to Buy Reebok for US $3.8 billion." *The New York Times: International Business*. August 3, 2005. https://www.nytimes.com/2005/08/03/business/worldbusiness/sportswear-maker-adidas-to-buy-reebok-for-us38.html.

Waller, Sam. "Interview: Joe Foster, Reebok Founder." *Oi Polloi* (blog). November 4, 2019. https://www.oipolloi.com/blogs/the-blog/interview-joe-foster-reebok-founder.

CHAPTER 4

Farfan, Barbara. "Quotes from Costco Founder James Sinegal: Quotations on Long-Term Success from a Successful Retail Leader." The Balance Small Business. Updated March 31, 2019.
https://www.thebalancesmb.com/quotes-on-leadership-costco-founder-james-sinegal-2892146.

Gallo, Amy. "The Value of Keeping the Right Customers." *Harvard Business Review.* October 29, 2014.
https://hbr.org/2014/10/the-value-of-keeping-the-right-customers.

Grossinger, Paul. "5 Fascinating Stats Show Purpose Transforming Work." *Inc.* September 22, 2020.
https://www.inc.com/paul-grossinger/5-fascinating-stats-show-purpose-transforming-work.html.

Swartz, John. "Amazon Is Officially Worth $1 Trillion, Joining Other Tech Titans." *MarketWatch.* February 4, 2020.
https://www.marketwatch.com/story/amazon-is-officially-worth-1-trillion-joining-other-tech-titans-2020-02-04.

TEDx UFM. "The Value of Asking Questions." November 2017. Video, 9:35.
https://www.ted.com/talks/karen_maeyens_the_value_of_asking_questions.

CHAPTER 5

"Michael E. Porter." Faculty & Research. Harvard Business School. Accessed June 5, 2020.
https://www.hbs.edu/faculty/Pages/profile.aspx?facId=6532.

Sage, Shannon. "Surprising Strategic Planning Stats." OnStrategy. Accessed June 17, 2020.
https://onstrategyhq.com/resources/surprising-strategic-planning-stats/.

SHEETZ. Accessed June 6, 2020.
https://www.sheetz.com.

Taylor, Kate. "Chick-fil-A Is the Third Largest Fast-Food Chain in America, and That Should Terrify Wendy's and Burger King." *Business Insider.* May 14, 2020.
https://www.businessinsider.com/chick-fil-a-third-largest-fast-food-chain-us-sales-2020-5.

CHAPTER 6

Goodreads. Cuschieri, David. Accessed June 19, 2020.
https://www.goodreads.com/quotes/9008454-the-mind-is-a-powerful-force-it-can-enslave-us.

CHAPTER 7

"2012: SpaceX: Elon Musk's Race to Space." *60 Minutes Rewind.* December 9, 2018. Video, 14:35.
https://www.youtube.com/watch?v=23GzpbNUyI4.

FWTX Staff. "Five Key Elements of Effective Leadership." *Fort Worth Magazine.* November 16, 2016. https://fwtx.com/news/voice/five-key-elements-effective-leadership/.

Howell, Elizabeth. "SpaceX: Facts about Elon Musk's Private Spaceflight Company." Space.com (Future US Inc,). December 16, 2019. https://www.space.com/18853-spacex.html.

Kane, Margaret. "eBay Picks up PayPal for $1.5 Billion." *CNET.* August 18, 2002. https://www.cnet.com/news/iphone-12-preorders-are-now-live-prices-release-dates-and-how-to-buy-apples-4-new-phones/.

CHAPTER 8

Boris, Vanessa." "What Makes Storytelling So Effective for Learning?" *Harvard Business Publishing.* December 20, 2017. https://www.harvardbusiness.org/what-makes-storytelling-so-effective-for-learning.

Dicks, Matthew. *Storyworthy.* California: New World Library, 2018.

Dosch, Kristi. "Already, Loyola And Villanova Have Seen Benefits From Basketball Success." *Forbes.* June 25, 2018. https://www.forbes.com/sites/kristidosh/2018/06/25/loyola-and-villanovas-basketball-success-positively-impacts-both-universities-for-years-to-come/#10354d921e52.

Friedman, Karen. "Primary Source: The Power of Storytelling in Business." *Public Relations Society of America, Inc.* February 1, 2018. https://apps.prsa.org/StrategiesTactics/Articles/view/12169/1154/Primary_Source_The_Power_of_Storytelling_in_Busine#.X4XDyC2ZOu5.

Hall, Kindra. *Stories That Stick.* Tennessee: HarperCollins Leadership, 2019. Page 199.

Hall, Kindra. *Stories That Stick.* Tennessee: HarperCollins Leadership, 2019. Page 63.

Harrison, Kate. "A Good Presentation Is about Data and Story." *Forbes.* January 20, 2015. https://www.forbes.com/sites/kateharrison/2015/01/20/a-good-presentation-is-about-data-and-story/#2512647c450f.

Janower, Jacob. "NCAA Tournament wins by coach: Most national championships in March Madness history." Sporting News. March 16, 2019. https://www.sportingnews.com/us/ncaa-basketball/news/ncaa-tournament-wins-by-coach-most-national-championships-in-march-madness-history/1kcody9jkhhbo155300yaojtrx#:~:text=Only%20three%20active%20coaches%20—%20MIke,who%20is%20atop%20the%20leaderboard.

CHAPTER 9

Chaffey, Dave. "Amazon.com marketing strategy: A business case study." Smart Insights. October 14, 2020. https://www.smartinsights.com/digital-marketing-strategy/online-business-revenue-models/amazon-case-study/

Guerra, Jennifer. "Borders Closing Its Bookstores after 40 Years." *NPR: Public Broadcasting.* July 19, 2011.
https://www.npr.org/2011/07/19/138499967/mich-book-chain-borders-closing-after-40-years.

Hartmans, Avery and Matt Weinberger. "Steve Jobs Would Have Been 65 on Monday." *Business Insider.* February 24, 2020.
https://www.businessinsider.com/steve-jobs-apple-photos-2017-1.

Husain, Shezray, Feroz Khan, and Waqas Mirza. "Brewing Innovation." *Business Today.* September 28, 2014.
https://www.businesstoday.in/magazine/lbs-case-study/how-starbucks-survived-the-financial-meltdown-of-2008/story/210059.html#:~:text=This%20was%20one%20of%20the,the%20same%20period%20in%202007.

Newman, Daniel. "Secret to Digital Transformation Success: Fail Fast to Innovate Faster." *Forbes.* May 16, 2017.
https://www.forbes.com/sites/danielnewman/2017/05/16/secret-to-digital-transformation-success-fail-fast-to-innovate-faster/#316b23c66907.

Nolan, Katie. "9 Iconic American Brands That No Longer Exist." Bob Vila: Action Media, Inc. Accessed September 21, 2020.

"Patriots Are Now 74-0 When Leading at Halftime at Home in the Regular Season Since 2002." Reddit. Reposted Twitter Image. NFL on ESPN Twitter: November 24, 2015. .
https://www.reddit.com/r/Patriots/comments/3u32d8/patriots_are_now_740_when_leading_at_halftime_at/.

United States Navy: Blue Angels Website. Accessed September 4, 2020.
https://www.blueangels.navy.mil.

CHAPTER 10

Gunnars, Kris. "Good Carbs, Bad Carbs — How to Make the Right Choices." *Healthline.* August 18, 2016.
https://www.healthline.com/nutrition/good-carbs-bad-carbs#:~:text=Carbs%20Are%20Not%20"Essential%2C",of%20carbohydrate%20in%20the%20diet.

Hyman, Dr. Mark. *Fat Fiction.* Prime Video. 2020